H. T. Crossley

Songs of Salvation as Used by Crossley and Hunter in Evangelistic Meetings

H. T. Crossley

Songs of Salvation as Used by Crossley and Hunter in Evangelistic Meetings

ISBN/EAN: 9783337254421

Printed in Europe, USA, Canada, Australia, Japan

Cover: Foto ©Lupo / pixelio.de

More available books at **www.hansebooks.com**

Fraternally
H. T. Crossley

Cordially
J. E. Hunter

Songs of Salvation

AS USED BY

CROSSLEY AND HUNTER,

IN EVANGELISTIC MEETINGS,

AND ADAPTED FOR THE

Church, Grove, School, Choir & Home

EDITED BY

REV. H. T. CROSSLEY.

PRICE { BOARDS, 35c. EACH. PER DOZEN, $3.60.
       { MANILLA, 25c.   "   "   2.50.

TORONTO:
WILLIAM BRIGGS, 78 & 80 KING ST. EAST.
MONTREAL: C. W. COATES.   HALIFAX: S. F. HUESTIS.
1887.

Entered, according to the Act of the Parliament of Canada, in the year one thousand eight hundred and eighty-seven, by H. T. CROSSLEY, in the Office of the Minister of Agriculture, at Ottawa.

PREFACE.

In preparing SONGS OF SALVATION, the following objects were kept in view :—

First, to have in one book the best of the songs we have tested, as particularly adapted for our Evangelistic Work.

Second, to provide a suitable book for Special Services, Prayer and Social Meetings, thus filling a long-felt want of pastors and churches.

Third, to supply the demand of Choirs for a book of the choicest Gospel Songs, for use after prayer and sermon in our church services.

Fourth, to furnish superintendents with a collection of songs, differing from the ordinary style of Sabbath-school music, that will be appreciated, and sung with a new spirit and interest.

Fifth, to give to parents a music book that may profitably be used in family worship, as well as being a parlor favorite.

Sixth, to please my numerous friends who have so frequently requested me to publish many of the songs I sing in Evangelistic Meetings.

Seventh, to meet the desire of lovers of music generally, to have a book full of the best sacred songs, new and old, instead of containing about half a dozen good pieces, and the others very ordinary.

PREFACE.

If the friends of Christian song believe I have attained the end desired, I shall be thankful, but if I have failed, it is not from want of expense, long and diligent research, and earnest endeavor. I have carefully examined over seventy-five music books, written the best composers for songs, and have selected those pieces I deemed the cream of the various publications. Several numbers were prepared especially for this work. The picture on the cover is of the Metropolitan Church, Toronto.

I hope and pray that these songs may help Christians Zionward, and win in the future, as in the past, many to love and trust Him, who loves us with His great heart of infinite love.

H. T. CROSSLEY.

NOTE.

The great majority of the songs in this book are copyright property, and, therefore, cannot honestly or honorably be used without permission.

Sing On—Concluded.

CHORUS.

Sing on; O, blissful music, With ev-'ry note you raise

My heart is filled with rap-ture, My soul is lost in praise.

Sing on; O, blissful music, With ev-'ry note you raise,
Sing on; blissful, blissful music,

My heart is filled with rap-ture, My soul is lost in praise.

Sing, O Sing the Love of Jesus—*Concluded.*

4   Whosoever.

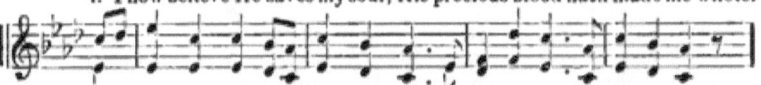

5   We Praise Thee.   Tune: G. H. & S. S., No. 24. Key G.

1 We praise Thee, O God, for the Son of Thy love,
   For Jesus who died, and is now gone above!

Cho.—Hallelujah! Thine the glory, Hallelujah! Amen.
   Hallelujah! Thine the glory, revive us again.

2 We praise Thee, O God! for Thy Spirit of light,
   Who has shown us our Saviour, and scattered our night.

3 All glory and praise to the Lamb that was slain,
   Who has borne all our sins, and has cleansed every stain.

4 All glory and praise to the God of all grace,
   Who has bought us, and sought us, and guided our ways.

5 Revive us again: fill each heart with Thy love;
   May each soul be rekindled with fire from above.

Seeking for Me.

L. E. Hasty.

1. Je-sus, my Saviour, to Beth-le-hem came, Born in a manger to
2. Je-sus, my Saviour, on Cal-va-ry's tree, Died for my sins, that my
3. Je-sus, my Saviour, the same as of old, While I did wan-der a-
4. Je-sus, my Saviour, shall come from on high, Sweet is the promise as

sorrow and shame; Oh, it was wonderful, blest be His name, Seeking for me, for
soul might be free; Oh, it was wonderful, how could it be? Dying for me, for
far from the fold, Gently and long He hath plead with my soul, Calling for me, for
wea-ry years fly; Oh, I shall see Him descending the sky, Coming for me, for

for me . . . . . for me . . . . .

me, Seeking for me, Seeking for me, Seeking for me, Seeking for me;
me, Dying for me, Dying for me, Dying for me, Dying for me;
me, Calling for me, Calling for me, Calling for me, Calling for me;
me, Coming for me, Coming for me, Coming for me, Coming for me;

Oh, it was wonderful, blest be His name, Seeking for me, for me.
Oh, it was wonderful, how could it be? Dying for me, for me.
Gently and long He hath plead with my soul, Calling for me, for me.
Oh, I shall see Him descending the sky, Coming for me, for me.

From "*Good Will*," by permission.   Copyright.

12. I Am Listening.

"It is the voice of my beloved that knocketh, saying, Open to me."—Cant. 5: 2.

W. S. MARSHALL.   W. S. MARSHALL.

1. Do you hear the Sav-iour call-ing, By the woo-ings of His
2. By His Spir-it He is woo-ing, Soft-ly draw-ing us to
3. By the Word of Truth He's speaking, To the wand'ring, err-ing
4. In His Pro-vi-den-tial dealings, E-ven in His stern de-

voice? Do you hear the accents falling? Will you make the precious choice?
Him, Thro' the day and night pursuing, With His gen-tle voice to win.
ones; List! the voice the stillness breaking! Hear the sweet and solemn tones!
crees, In the loudest thunders peal-ing, Or the murm'ring of the breeze.

REFRAIN.

I am list-'ning, Oh, I'm list-'ning, Just to hear the ac-cents

Repeat softly.

fall; I am list'ning, Oh, I'm list'ning, To the Saviour's loving call.

From "*Spiritual Songs.*"

13. Hark! There Comes a Whisper.

FANNY J. CROSBY.   *Prov. 23: 26.*   W. H. DOANE.

1. Hark! there comes a whisper Stealing on thine ear; 'Tis the Saviour calling, Soft, soft and clear,
2. With that voice so gentle, Dost thou hear Him say, Tell Me all thy sorrows, Come, come away?
3. Wouldst thou find a refuge For thy soul oppressed? Jesus kindly answers, I am thy rest.
4. At the cross of Je-sus Let thy burden fall, While He gently whispers, I'll bear it all.

REFRAIN. Give thy heart to Me, Once I died for thee; Hark! hark! thy Saviour calls, Come, sin-ner, come. Just now, O come,

By permission.

14. Precious Jesus.

TUNE: "I AM LISTENING."

1 Precious Jesus, oh! to love Thee,
   Oh! to know that Thou art mine;
Jesus, all my heart I give Thee,
   If Thou wilt but make it Thine.

CHORUS.

I am listening just to hear the accents fall;
I am listening to the Saviour's loving call.

2 Take my warmest, best affections,
   Take my memory, mind and will;
Then with all Thy loving Spirit
   All my emptied nature fill.

3 Bold I touch Thy sacred garment,
   Trusting stretch my eager hand;
Virtue, like a healing fountain,
   Freely flows at love's command.

4 Oh, how precious, dear Redeemer,
   Is the love that fills my soul!
It is done, the word is spoken,
   Be thou every whit made whole.

5 Lo! a new creation dawning;
   Lo! I rise to life divine;
In my soul an Easter morning;
   I am Christ's, and Christ is mine.

15. He Loved Me So

E. O. E.   "God so loved the world."—John 3:16.   E. O. Excell.

1. By faith the Lamb of God I see, Expiring on the cross for me;
   He paid the mighty debt I owe; He died because He loved me so.
2. For me the Father sent His Son; For me the victory He won;
   To save my soul from endless woe, He died because He loved me so.
3. So glad I am that He is mine, So glad that I with Him shall shine;
   I'll trust in Him, for this I know, He died because He loved me so.
4. O Lamb of God that made me free, I consecrate my all to Thee;
   My all,—for this I surely know, He died because He loved me so.
5. And when my Lord shall bid me come, To join the loved ones round the throne,
   I'll sing, as through the gates I go, He died because He loved me so.

REFRAIN.
He loved me so, he loved me so, He died because He loved me so
He loved.

From "The Gospel in Song," by permission.   Copyright.

16. Jesus of Nazareth Passeth By.

TUNE: G. H. & S. S., No. 8. KEY G.

1. What means this eager, anxious throng,
Which moves with busy haste along—
These wondrous gatherings day by day?
What means this strange commotion, [pray?
: In accents hush'd the throng reply :
"Jesus of Nazareth passeth by." :||

2. Who is this Jesus? Why should He
The city move so mightily?
A passing stranger, has He skill
To move the multitude at will?
||: Again the stirring notes reply:
"Jesus of Nazareth passeth by." :||

3. Again He comes! From place to place
His holy footprints we can trace.
He pauseth at our threshold—nay,
He enters—condescends to stay.
||: Shall we not gladly raise the cry—
"Jesus of Nazareth passeth by?" :||

4. Ho! all ye heavy laden, come:
Here's pardon, comfort, rest and home.
Ye wanderers from a Father's face,
Return, accept His proffered grace.
||: Ye tempted ones, there's refuge nigh—
"Jesus of Nazareth passeth by!" :||

17. The Glorious Fountain.

"In that day there shall be a fountain opened . . . for sin and uncleanness."—*Zech.* 13: 1.

COWPER. T. C. O'KANE.

1. { There is a fountain filled with blood, Filled with blood, filled with blood, There
     And sinners plunged beneath that flood, Beneath that flood, beneath that flood,
   [And is a fountain filled with blood Drawn from Im-man-uel's veins;
    sinners plunged beneath that flood Lose all their guil-ty stains. }

CHORUS.
Oh, glo-ri-ous foun-tain! Here will I stay, . . .
And in Thee ev-er Wash my sins a-way!

2 The dying thief rejoiced to see
   That fountain in his day;
   And there may I, though vile as he,
   Wash all my sins away.

3 Thou dying Lamb, Thy precious
      blood
   Shall never lose its power,
   Till all the ransomed Church of God
   Are saved, to sin no more.

4 E'er since, by faith, I saw the stream
   Thy flowing wounds supply,
   Redeeming love has been my theme,
   And shall be till I die.

5 Then in a nobler, sweeter song
   I'll sing Thy power to save,
   When this poor lisping, stammering
      tongue,
   Lies silent in the grave.

By permission.

21. The Crucifixion.

I. Watts.
Tune: No. 20.

1 When I survey the wondrous cross
 On which the Prince of glory died,
My richest gain I count but loss,
 And pour contempt on all my pride.

Chorus.
O Calvary! dark Calvary!
My longing heart is turned to thee;
O Calvary! dark Calvary!
Speak to my heart from Calvary.

2 Forbid it, Lord, that I should boast,
 Save in the death of Christ, my God:
All the vain things that charm me most,
 I sacrifice them to His blood.

3 See, from His head, His hands, His feet,
 Sorrow and love flow mingled down;
Did e'er such love and sorrow meet,
 Or thorns compose so rich a crown?

4 Were the whole realm of nature mine,
 That were a present far too small;
Love so amazing, so divine,
 Demands my soul, my life, my all.

22. Galilee.

Tune: No. 20.

1 O Galilee, sweet Galilee,
 What memories rise at thought of thee;
In mortal guise upon thy shore
 The Saviour trod whom we adore.

Chorus.
O Galilee, sweet Galilee,
Thy blessed name will sacred be
In ev'ry clime, on ev'ry shore,
Till suns shall rise and set no more.

2 Thy waves which once his vessel bore
 Will sound His praise forever more,
And from thy depths, beloved sea,
 We hear His call of "Follow Me."

3 Thro' ages yet to come thy name
 A homage true will ever claim;
'Tis hallowed ground where once He trod,
 The Prince of Peace, the Son of God.

23. Tell Me More About Jesus.

P. P. Bliss.
James McGranahan.

1 'Tis known on earth and heaven too
 'Tis sweet to me because 'tis true,
The "old, old story" is ever new;
 Tell me more about Jesus.

Chorus.
"Tell me more about Jesus!"
"Tell me more about Jesus!"
Him would I know who loved me so;
 "Tell me more about Jesus!"

2 Earth's fairest flowers will droop and die,
 Dark clouds o'erspread yon azure sky;
Life's dearest joys flit swiftly by:
 Tell me more about Jesus.

3 When overwhelmed with unbelief,
 When burdened with a blinding grief,
Come kindly then to my relief;
 Tell me more about Jesus.

4 And when the Glory-land I see,
 And take the "place prepared" for me,
Through endless years my song shall be—
 Tell me more about Jesus.

26. Gethsemane.

REV. E. P. HAMMOND. OLD MELODY. Arranged.

1. My Jesus, I would ne'er forget That hour I spent with Thee;
CHORUS.—I'll ne'er forget, I'll ne'er forget, I'll ne'er forgetful be,
When there I saw Thy bloody sweat, In dark Gethsemane.
When there I saw Thy bloody sweat, In dark Gethsemane.

2 'Twas in that olive press I felt
  That Thou didst bleed for me;
Alas! how great I saw my guilt
  While in Gethsemane.
3 'Twas there I felt my guilt and shame
  In oft forsaking Thee,

How precious was Thy very name
  In dear Gethsemane.
4 Should e'er our love to Thee grow cold
  And we forgetful be,
We'll call to mind Thy love untold
  While in Gethsemane.

27 Christ's Vicarious Sacrifice.
I. WATTS.   TUNE: "Gethsemane."

1 Alas! and did my Saviour bleed?
  And did my Sov'reign die?
Would He devote that sacred head
  For such a worm as I?
    CHORUS.
Help me, dear Saviour, Thee to own,
  And ever faithful be;
And as Thou sittest on Thy throne
  O "Lord, remember me."

2 Was it for crimes that I have done,
  He groan'd upon the tree?
Amazing pity! grace unknown!
  And love beyond degree!

3 Well might the sun in darkness
  hide,
And shut his glories in,
When Christ, the mighty Maker, died
  For man, the creature's sin.

4 Thus might I hide my blushing face,
  While His dear cross appears;
Dissolve my heart in thankfulness,
  And melt mine eyes to tears.

5 But drops of grief can ne'er repay
  The debt of love I owe;
Here, Lord, I give myself away,—
  'Tis all that I can do.

28 God Loved the World.
MRS. STOCKTON.   TUNE: "Gethsemane."

1 God loved the world of sinners lost
  And ruined by the fall;
Salvation full, at highest cost,
  He offers free to all.
    CHORUS.
Oh, it was love, 'twas wondrous love!
  The love of God to me;
It brought my Saviour from above
  To die on Calvary.

2 E'en now by faith I claim Him mine,
  The risen Son of God

Redemption by His death I find,
  And cleansing through His blood.
3 Love brings the glorious fulness in,
  And to His saints makes known
The blessed rest from inbred sin,
  Through faith in Christ alone.

4 Of victory now o'er Satan's power,
  Let all the ransomed sing
And triumph, in the dying hour,
  Through Christ, the Lord, our King.

29. Rock of Ages.

A. M. Toplady.   Thos. Hastings.

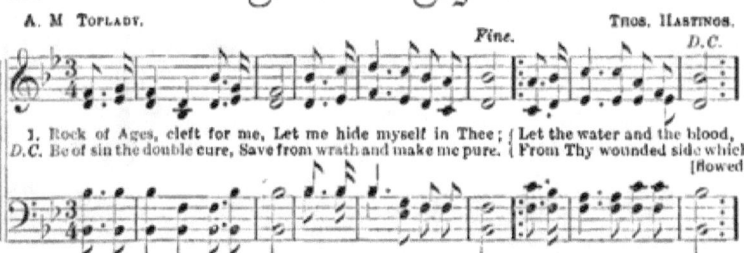

1. Rock of Ages, cleft for me, Let me hide myself in Thee; { Let the water and the blood,
D.C. Be of sin the double cure, Save from wrath and make me pure. { From Thy wounded side which
[flowed,

2. Could my tears forever flow,
   Could my zeal no languor know,
   These for sin could not atone;
   Thou must save, and Thou alone;
   In my hand no price I bring;
   Simply to Thy cross I cling.

3. While I draw this fleeting breath,
   When my eyes shall close in death,
   When I rise to worlds unknown,
   And behold Thee on Thy throne,
   Rock of Ages, cleft for me,
   Let me hide myself in Thee.

30. Jesus "Lifted Up."

I, if I be lifted up from the earth, will draw all men unto Me.
—*John 12: 32.*

Anna Warner.   W. B. Bradbury.

1. Jesus, from His throne on high, Came in-to this world to die—
   That I might from sin be free, Bled and died up-on the tree.
2. I can see Him e-ven now, With His pierced, thorn-clad brow,
   A-gon-iz-ing on the tree, Oh, what love, and all for me!
3. Je-sus loves me!—He who died Heaven's gates to o-pen wide!
   He will wash a-way my sin, Let His lit-tle child come in.
4. Now I feel this heart of stone Drawn to love God's ho-ly Son,
   "Lifted up" on Cal-va-ry, Suffering death and shame for me.
5. Je-sus, take this heart of mine; Make it pure and whol-ly Thine;
   Thou hast bled and died for me, I will henceforth live for Thee

CHORUS.

1st Cho.—Yes, Jesus loves me! Yes, Jesus loves me! Yes, Jesus loves me! The Bible tells me so.
2nd Cho.—Yes, I love Jesus! Yes, I love Jesus! Yes, I love Jesus! I know, I know, I do.
3rd Cho.—I would love Jesus! I would love Jesus! I would love Jesus! Because He died for me.

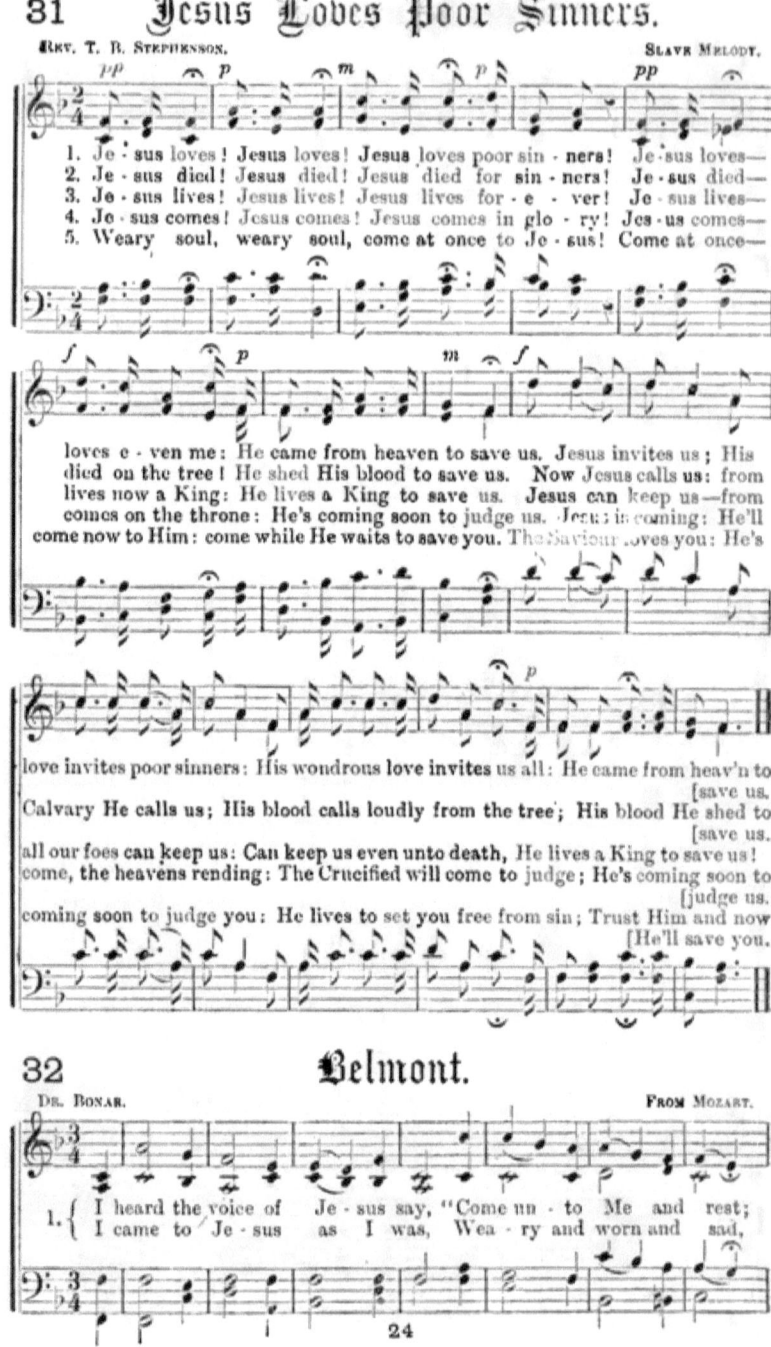

Belmont—Concluded.

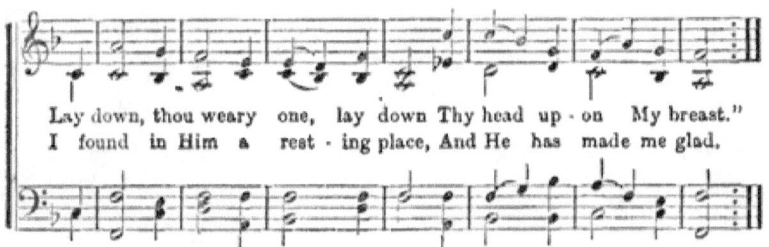

Lay down, thou weary one, lay down Thy head up-on My breast."
I found in Him a rest-ing place, And He has made me glad.

CHORUS.
Come away, come away,
Come away to Jesus;
Come away, come away home,
For Jesus waits to save you.

2 I heard the voice of Jesus say,
"Behold, I freely give
The living water; thirsty one,
Stoop down, and drink, and live."
I came to Jesus, and I drank
Of that life-giving stream:

My thirst was quenched, my soul revived,
And now I live in Him.

3 I heard the voice of Jesus say,
"I am this dark world's Light;
Look unto Me, thy morn shall rise,
And all thy day be bright."
I looked to Jesus, and I found
In Him my Star, my Sun;
And in that Light of life I'll walk
Till travelling days are done.

33 Return, O Wanderer.

TUNE: "Belmont" and "Jesus Loves."

1 Return, O wanderer, to thy home,
Thy Father calls for thee;
No longer now an exile roam,
In guilt and misery.

CHORUS.
Steal away, steal away,
Steal away to Jesus;
Steal away, steal away home,
You've not got long to stay here.

2 Return, O wanderer, to thy home,
'Tis Jesus calls for thee;
The Spirit and the Bride say, Come;
Oh, now for refuge flee.

3 There Jesus stands with open arms;
He calls—He bids you come:
Though guilt restrains and fear alarms,
Behold, there yet is room.

4 Return, O wanderer, to thy home,
'Tis madness to delay;
There are no pardons in the tomb,
And brief is mercy's day.

5 Oh, come, and with His children taste
The blessings of His love;
While hope expects the sweet repast
Of sweeter joys above

34 The Coming Bridegroom.

Arranged.   TUNE: "Redeeming Love" 58.

1 ‖: Are you ready for the Bridegroom
    When He comes, when He comes? :‖
Behold! He cometh! behold! He cometh! [groom comes.
Be robed and ready, for the Bride-

CHORUS.
‖: Behold the Bridegroom, for He comes,
    for He comes! :‖   [cometh!
Behold! He cometh! behold! He
Be robed and ready, for the Bride-
    groom comes.

2 ‖: We will all go out to meet Him
    When He comes, when He comes; :‖
He surely cometh! He surely cometh!
We'll go to meet Him when the Bridegroom comes.

3 ‖: We will chant alleluias
    When He comes, when He comes; :‖
Lo! soon He cometh! Lo! soon He cometh!
Sing alleluia! for the Bridegroom comes.

35. Jesus Saves.

PRISCILLA J. OWENS.   WM. J. KIRKPATRICK, by per.

1. We have heard a joyful sound, Jesus saves, Jesus saves;
Spread the gladness all around, Jesus saves, Jesus saves;
Bear the news to ev'ry land, Climb the steeps and cross the waves;
Onward, 'tis our Lord's command, Jesus saves, Jesus saves.

2 Waft it on the rolling tide,
  Jesus saves, Jesus saves;
Tell to sinners far and wide,
  Jesus saves, Jesus saves;
Sing, ye islands of the sea,
Echo back, ye ocean caves,
Earth shall keep her jubilee,
  Jesus saves, Jesus saves.

3 Sing above the battle's strife
  Jesus saves, Jesus saves;
By His death and endless life
  Jesus saves, Jesus saves;
Sing it softly thro' the gloom,
When the heart for mercy craves,
Sing in triumph o'er the tomb,
  Jesus saves, Jesus saves.

36   I Gave My Life.
MISS HAVERGAL.   (G. H. 21.)

37   I Hear Thy Welcome Voice.
L. HARTSOUGH.   (G. H. 63.)

1 I gave My life for thee,
  My precious blood I shed,
That thou might'st ransomed be
  And quickened from the dead;
I gave, I gave My life for thee,
What hast thou given for Me?

2 And I have brought to thee,
  Down from My home above,
Salvation full and free,
  My pardon and My love;
I bring, I bring rich gifts to thee,
What hast thou brought to Me?

3 Oh, let thy life be given,
  Thy years for Him be spent;
Sin's fetters all be riven,
  And joy with suffering blent.
I gave, I gave Myself for thee,
Give thou thyself to Me.

1 I hear Thy welcome voice,
  That calls me, Lord, to Thee,
For cleansing in Thy precious blood,
  That flowed on Calvary.

CHORUS.
I am coming, Lord,
  Coming now to Thee!
Wash me, cleanse me in the blood
  That flowed on Calvary.

2 'Tis Jesus calls me on
  To perfect faith and love,
To perfect hope, and peace, and trust,
  For earth and heaven above.

3 And He the witness gives
  To loyal hearts and free,
That every promise is fulfilled,
  If faith but brings the plea.

4 All hail, atoning blood!
  All hail, redeeming grace!
All hail, the gift of Christ our Lord,
  Our Strength and Righteousness!

38   Coronation.
REV. EDWARD PERRONET.   (G. H. 101.)

1 All hail the power of Jesus' name!
    Let angels prostrate fall;
    Bring forth the royal diadem,
    And crown Him Lord of all.

2 Sinners, whose love can ne'er forget
    The wormwood and the gall;
    Go, spread your trophies at His feet
    And crown Him Lord of all.

3 Let every kindred, every tribe,
    On this terrestrial ball,
    To Him all majesty ascribe,
    And crown Him Lord of all.

4 O that with yonder sacred throng
    We at His feet may fall;
    We'll join the everlasting song,
    And crown Him Lord of all.

39   My Redeemer.
P. P. BLISS.   (G. H. 229.)

1 I will sing of my Redeemer,
    And His wondrous love to me;
    On the cruel cross He suffered,
    From the curse to set me free.

CHORUS.

Sing, oh, sing of my Redeemer,
    And His wondrous love to me;
    On the cross He bought my pardon,
    Jesus saves me, I am free.

2 I will tell the wondrous story,
    How, my lost estate to save,
    In His boundless love and mercy,
    He the ransom freely gave.

3 I will praise my dear Redeemer,
    His triumphant power I'll tell,
    How the victory He giveth
    Over sin, and death, and hell.

4 I will sing of my Redeemer,
    And His heavenly love to me;
    He from death to life hath brought me,
    Son of God, with Him to be.

40   The Bleeding Lamb.
E. P. HAMMOND.   TUNE: H. S. 63.

1 Jesus Christ has bled and died,
    Glory to the bleeding Lamb!
    He for our sins was crucified,
    Hallelujah to the Lamb!

CHORUS.   [Lamb!

The Lamb, the Lamb, the bleeding
    I love the sound of Jesus' name;
    It sets my spirit in a flame,
    Glory to the bleeding Lamb.

2 And now from sin we may be free,
    Glory to the bleeding Lamb!
    He offers peace to you and me,
    Hallelujah to the Lamb!

3 I know my sins are all forgiven,
    Glory to the bleeding Lamb!
    And I am on my way to heaven,
    Hallelujah to the Lamb!

4 We now will sing the Saviour's praise,
    Glory to the bleeding Lamb!
    Him will we serve throughout our days,
    Hallelujah to the Lamb!

5 And when the voyage of life is o'er,
    Glory to the bleeding Lamb!
    I'll sing upon a happier shore,
    Hallelujah to the Lamb!

41   The Great Physician.
REV. WM. HUNTER   (G. H. 56.)

1 The great Physician now is near,
    The sympathizing Jesus;
    He speaks the drooping heart to cheer,
    Oh, hear the voice of Jesus.

CHORUS.

Sweetest note in seraph song,
    Sweetest name on mortal tongue,
    Sweetest carol ever sung,
    Jesus, blessed Jesus.

2 All glory to the dying Lamb!
    I now believe in Jesus;
    I love the blessed Saviour's name,
    I love the name of Jesus.

3 His name dispels my guilt and fear,
    No other name but Jesus;
    Oh, how my soul delights to hear
    The precious name of Jesus.

4 And when to that bright world above,
    We rise to see our Jesus,
    We'll sing around the throne of love
    His name, the name of Jesus.

Mercy is Boundless and Free—*Concluded.*

D.C. Refrain.

Life everlast-ing thy soul may receive, Mercy is boundless and free.
Jesus is waiting, He'll save you to-night, Mercy is boundless and free.
Grieve Him no longer, but come as thou art, Mercy is boundless and free.
Cling to His mercy, believe on His name, Mercy is boundless and free.

43 Jesus Bids You Come.

W. L. T. W. L. THOMPSON.

1. Jesus bids you come, Jesus bids you come, Now for you He's interceding,
2. Jesus bids you come, Jesus bids you come, Weary trav'ler, do not tarry,
3. Jesus bids you come, Jesus bids you come, Voices may not always call you,
4. Jesus bids you come, Jesus bids you come, Where 'tis love and joy forever,

Gently at thy heart He's pleading, "Come unto Me, Come unto Me"
Je - sus will thy burdens carry, Oh, will you come? Oh, will you come?
"Late, too late," may yet befall you, "Why will ye die?" "Why will ye die?
Where we'll meet to part, no, never, Sinner, come home, Oh, come, come home.

By permission of W. L. Thompson & Co. Copyright.

44 Seeking to Save.

P. P. BLISS. (G. H. 177.)

1 Tenderly the Shepherd,
  O'er the mountains cold,
  Goes to bring His lost one
  Back to the fold.

CHORUS.

:Seeking to save, seeking to save,
Lost one, 'tis Jesus seeking to save.:

2 Patiently the Spirit
  Seeks with earnest care,
  In the dust and darkness,
  His treasure rare.

3 Lovingly the Father
  Sends the news around,
  He once dead now liveth,
  Once lost is found.

45. Jesus is Calling.

W. L. T.
Will L. Thompson.

1. Soft-ly and ten-der-ly Jesus is calling, Calling for you and for me;
2. Why should we tarry when Jesus is pleading, Pleading for you and for me?
3. Time is now fleeting, the moments are passing, Passing from you and from me;
4. Oh! for the wonderful love He has promised, Promised for you and for me;

See on the portals He's waiting and watching, Watching for you and for me.
Why should we linger and heed not His mercies, Mercies for you and for me?
Shadows are gathering, death beds are coming, Coming for you and for me.
Tho' we have sinned He has mercy and pardon, Pardon for you and for me.

CHORUS:

Come home, . come home, Ye who are wea-ry, come home;
Come home, come home,

Earnestly, tenderly Je-sus is calling, Calling, O sinner, come home!

By permission. Copyright.

Pleading with Thee—Concluded.

53. Jesus Will Give You Rest.

FANNY J. CROSBY.   JOHN R. SWENEY.

1. Will you come, will you come, with your poor broken heart, Burden'd and sin-op-
2. Will you come, will you come? there is mercy for you, Balm for your aching
3. Will you come, will you come? you have nothing to pay; Jesus, who loves you
4. Will you come, will you come? how He pleads with you now! Fly to His loving

pressed? Lay it down at the feet of your Saviour and Lord,
breast; On-ly come as you are, and believe on His name,
best, By His death on the Cross purchased life for your soul,
breast; And what-ev-er your sin or your sor-row may be,

Je-sus will give you rest.

REFRAIN.

Oh, hap-py rest! sweet hap-py rest! Je-sus will give you rest, Oh! why won't you come in sim-ple, trust-ing faith? Je-sus will give you rest.

From "*Joy to the World*," by permission.   Copyright.

54. Only Trust Him.

J. H. S.   Rev. J. H. Stockton, by per.

1. Come, ev-'ry soul by sin oppress'd, There's mercy with the Lord: And He will surely give you rest, By trust-ing in His word.

CHORUS.
On-ly trust Him, on-ly trust Him, On-ly trust Him now; He will save you, He will save you, He will save you now.

2 For Jesus shed His precious blood,
   Rich blessings to bestow;
Plunge now into the crimson flood
   That washes white as snow.

3 Yes, Jesus is the truth, the way
   That leads you into rest;
Believe in Him without delay,
   And you are fully blest.

4 O Jesus, blessed Jesus, dear,
   I'm coming now to Thee;
Since Thou hast made the way so clear,
   And full salvation free.

5 Come, then, and join this holy band
   And on to glory go;
To dwell in that celestial land,
   Where joys immortal flow.

55   Come, Humble Sinner.

Ed. Jones. Changed by H. T. C.   Tune: No. 54.

1 Come, halting sinner, in whose breast
   A thousand thoughts revolve;
Come with your guilt and fear oppressed
   And make this last resolve.

Chorus.
Come to Jesus, come believing,
   Come to Jesus now;
He will save you, He will save you,
   He will save you now.

2 I'll go to Jesus, though my sins
   Like mountains round me close;
I know His courts; I'll enter in,
   Whatever may oppose.

3 He surely will admit my plea,
   He now will hear my prayer;
I cannot perish if I pray,
   For none have perished there.

4 I cannot perish if I go—
   I'll call "while He is nigh;"
For if I stay away, I know
   I must forever die.

56   O What Amazing Words of Grace!

Tune: No. 54.

1 O what amazing words of grace
   Are in the Gospel found!
Suited to every sinner's case,
   Who knows the joyful sound.

Chorus.
Come to Jesus, come believing,
   Come to Jesus now;
He will save you, He will save you,
   He will save you now.

2 Poor, sinful, thirsty, fainting souls,
   Are freely welcome here;
Salvation, like a river, rolls,
   Abundant, free, and clear.

3 Come, then, with all your wants and wounds;
   Your every burden bring;
Here love, unchanging love, abounds,
   A deep, celestial spring.

4 Whoever will—O gracious word!—
   May of this stream partake;
Come, thirsty souls, and bless the Lord,
   And drink, for Jesus' sake.

58. Let Him In.

Rev. J. B. Atchinson. E. O. Excell.

1. There's a Stranger at the door, Let Him in,
2. Open now to Him your heart, Let Him in,
3. Hear you now His loving voice? Let Him in,
4. Now admit the heavenly Guest, Let Him in,

Let the Saviour in, let the Saviour in,

He has been there oft before, Let Him in;
If you wait He will de-part, Let Him in;
Now, oh, now make Him your choice, Let Him in,
He will make for you a feast, Let Him in,

Let the Saviour in, let the Saviour in,

Let Him in ere He is gone, Let Him in, the Ho-ly One, Je-sus
Let Him in, He is your friend, He your soul will sure defend, He will
He is standing at the door, Joy to you He will restore, And His
He will speak your sins forgiven, And when earth ties all are riven, He will

Christ, the Father's Son, Let Him in.
keep you to the end, Let Him in.
name you will adore, Let Him in.
take you home to heaven, Let Him in.

Let the Saviour in, let the Saviour in.

From "*The Gospel in Song*," by permission. Copyright

59. Tell it to Jesus.

J. E. Rankin, D.D. — Matt. 14:12. — E. S. Lorenz.

1. Are you wea-ry, are you heav-y hearted? Tell it to Je-sus,
2. Do the tears flow down your cheeks unbidden? Tell it to Je-sus,
3. Do you fear the gath'ring clouds of sorrow? Tell it to Je-sus,
4. Are you trou-bled at the thought of dy-ing? Tell it to Je-sus,

Tell it to Je-sus. Are you grieving ov-er joys de-part-ed?
Tell it to Je-sus. Have you sins that to man's eye are hid-den?
Tell it to Je-sus. Are you anxious what shall be to-morrow?
Tell it to Je-sus. For Christ's coming Kingdom are you sigh-ing?

CHORUS.

Tell it to Je-sus a-lone. Tell it to Je-sus, Tell it to Jesus, He is a friend well known: You have no other such a friend or broth-er, Tell it to Je-sus a-lone.

From "*Songs of Refreshing*," by permission. Copyright

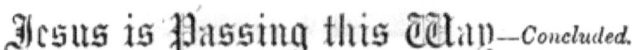

Jesus is Passing this Way—Concluded.

While He is near, O be-lieve Him, Open your heart to receive Him, For

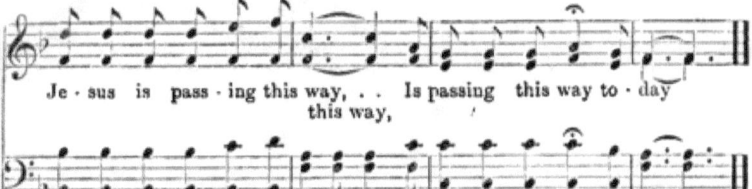

Je-sus is pass-ing this way, . . Is passing this way to-day
this way,

61 Are You Coming Home?
A. N. (G. H. 311.)

1 Are you coming home, ye wanderers,
   Whom Jesus died to win,
   All footsore, lame and weary,
   Your garments stained with sin?
   Will you seek the blood of Jesus
   To wash your garments white?
   Will you trust His precious promise,
   Are you coming home to-night?

CHORUS.
‖:Are you coming home to-night, :‖
   Are you coming home to Jesus,
   Out of darkness into light?
‖:Are you coming home to-night, :‖
   To your loving, heavenly Father,
   Are you coming home to-night?

2 Are you coming home, ye guilty,
   Who bear the load of sin?
   Outside you've long been standing,
   Come now and venture in;
   Will you heed the Saviour's promise,
   And dare to trust Him quite?
   "Come unto Me," saith Jesus,
   Are you coming home to-night?

3 Are you coming home, ye lost ones?
   Behold your Lord doth wait;
   Come, then, no longer linger,
   Come ere it be too late;
   Will you come and let Him save you?
   Oh, trust His love and might;
   Will you come while He is calling,
   Are you coming home to night?

62 The Water of Life.
(D. H. 29.)

1 Jesus the water of life will give,
   Freely, freely, freely,
   Jesus the water of life will give,
   Freely to those that love Him.
   Come to the fountain, O drink and
        live,
   Freely, freely, freely,   [live,
   Come to that fountain, O drink and
   Flowing for those that love Him

CHORUS.
   The Spirit and the Bride say, Come,
   Freely, freely, freely,
   And he that is thirsty, let him come,
   And drink of the water of life.
   The fountain of life is flowing,
   Flowing, freely flowing,
   The fountain of life is flowing,
   Is flowing for you and for me.

2 Jesus has promised a home in heaven,
   Freely, freely, freely,
   Jesus has promised a home in heaven,
   Freely to those that love Him.
   Treasures unfading will there be given,
   Freely, freely, freely,
   Treasures unfading will there be given,
   Freely to those that love Him.

3 Jesus has promised a robe of white,
   Kingdoms of glory and crowns of light.

4 Jesus has promised eternal day,
   Pleasures that never shall pass away.

64. Ah, My Heart.

"Come unto Me, all ye that labor and are heavy laden."—Matt. 11:28.

JOHN M. NEALE.   Changed by H. T. C   P. P. BLISS, by per.

First Solo.

1. Ah, my heart is heav-y lad-en, Wea-ry and oppressed!
2. Hath He marks to lead me to Him, If He be my guide?
3. If I find Him, If I fol-low, What my por-tion here?
4. If I still hold close-ly to Him, What have I at last?
5. If I ask Him to re-ceive me, Will He say me nay?

Second Solo.

"Come to Me," saith One, "and com-ing, Be at rest!"
"In His feet and hands are wound-prints, And His side."
"Grace to con-quer, Christ to com-fort And to cheer."
"Peace in dy-ing, la-bor end-ed, Hea-ven's rest."
"Not till earth, and not till hea-ven Pass a-way."

CHORUS. *Repeat last two lines of each verse.*   *rit.*   *p*

"Come to Me," saith One, "and com-ing, Be at rest!"

65. Come to Jesus.

1. Come to Je-sus, Come to Je-sus, Come to Je-sus just now;
Just now come to Je-sus, Come to Je-sus just now.

2 He will save you.
3 Oh, believe Him.
4 He is able.
5 He is willing.
6 He'll receive you.
7 Call upon Him.
8 He'll forgive you.
9 Only trust Him.
10 Jesus loves you.
11 Don't reject Him.
12 I do trust Him.
13 Jesus save me.
14 I love Jesus.
15 Hallelujah, Amen.

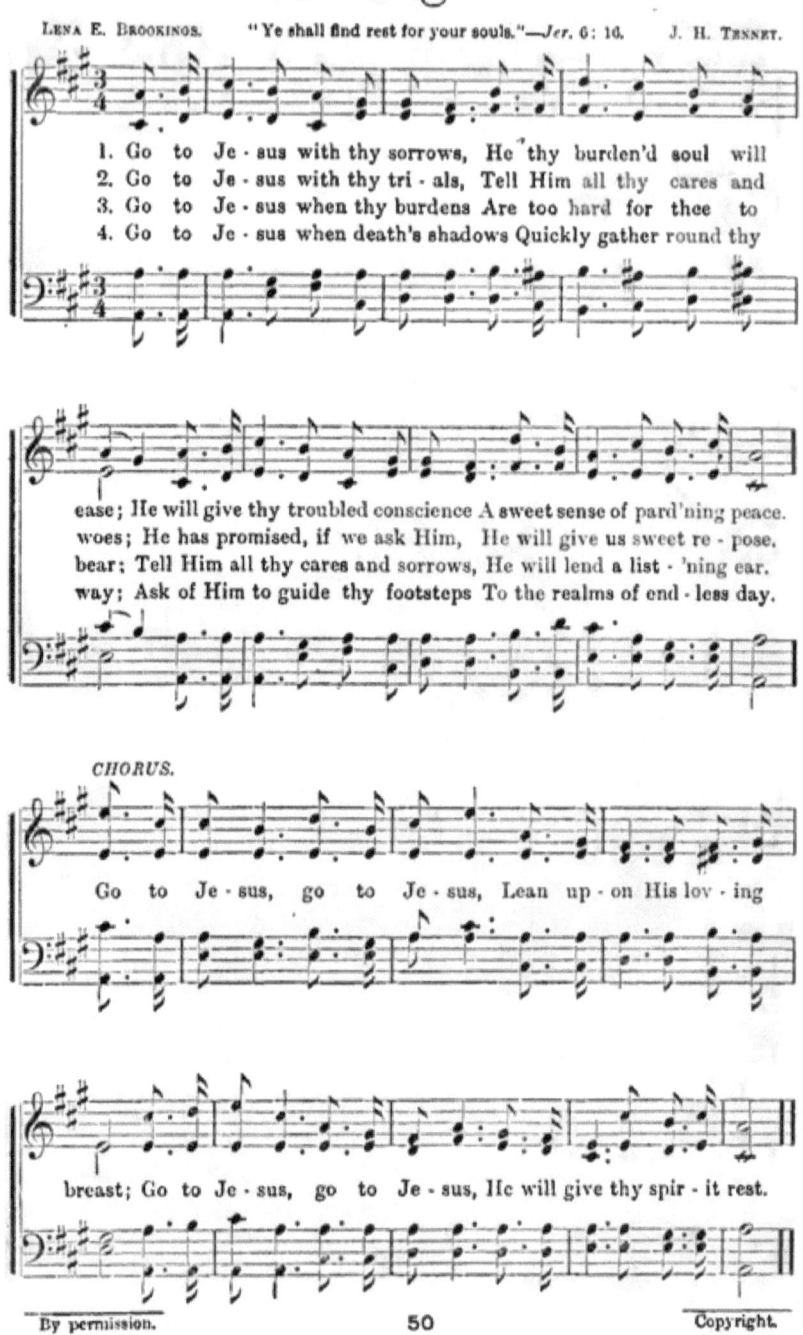

69. Look Away to the Cross.

Prof. I. E. Lehman. "Look unto Me, and be ye saved."—*Isa.* 45:22. I. Baltzell. Arranged.

1. Oh, have you not seen upon Calvary's brow, the cross where the Saviour hath died? 'Tis hallowed and blest by the presence of God, And stained by the blood from His side.
2. He died on the cross to atone for our sin—To purchase our pardon with blood; To o-pen a fountain for cleansing from sin, And seal us the children of God.
3. Oh, weary one, pressed by the weight of your sin, And longing from guilt to be free; Look up to the cross where the Saviour hath died; There are mercy and pardon for thee.
4. One look at the cross upon Calvary's brow—One look at that hallow-ed tree, Will bring to your soul the rich bless-ing of peace, Oh, look! sinner, look! and be free.

CHORUS.

Look away, . . . look away, . . . To the cross! To the cross! To the cross where the Saviour died! There is hope in the cross! There is cleansing from dross! There is life in the crim-son tide!

By permission.   Copyright.

Abundantly Able to Save—*Concluded.*

sinners He gave.   And He is a - bun - - dantly able to save.
ransom for sinners He gave,   And He is abundantly able to save.

71   **Jesus Will Forgive.**

Mrs. LOULA K. ROGERS.   R. M. McINTOSH.

1. Come, ye sinners, come to - day: Je - sus will for - give you free - ly.
2. Come un - to the mer - cy seat: Je - sus will for - give you free - ly.

All your sins He'll wash away: Je - sus will for - give you free - ly.
Humbly fall - ing at His feet: Je - sus will for - give you free - ly.

REFRAIN

O, come to - day! Why lon - ger stay a - way? He will not
say you nay: Je - sus will for - give you free - ly.

3 Lay your treasures up above:
   Jesus will forgive you freely.
  Trust the riches of His love:
   Jesus will forgive you freely

4 Earnestly a blessing seek:
   Jesus will forgive you freely.
  Trembling sinner, faint and weak,
   Jesus will forgive you freely.

5 He is able all to save:
   Jesus will forgive you freely.
  For your love His blood He gave:
   Jesus will forgive you freely.

6 Then, ye sinners, come to-day:
   Jesus will forgive you freely.
  All your sins He'll wash away:
   Jesus will forgive you freely.

From "*Prayer and Praise*," by permission.   Copyright.

God is Coming—*Concluded.*

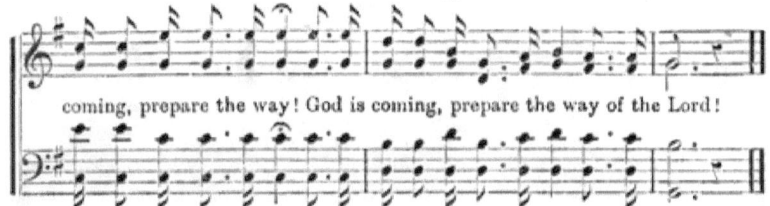

coming, prepare the way! God is coming, prepare the way of the Lord!

73 Jesus is Waiting to Save.

E. O. E. Arranged.   E. O. Excell. Arranged.

1. Why do you linger in darkness so long? Je-sus is waiting to save you!
2. Leave the broad road and the narrow way choose, Je-sus is waiting to save you!
3. Time will not lin-ger, how soon we must go! Je-sus is waiting to save you!
4. Je-sus is call-ing, "Oh, come un-to Me!" Je-sus is waiting to save you!
5. While we are pray-ing, oh, stay not a-way! Je-sus is waiting to save you!
    save you now!

Have you not friends in the heavenly throng? Je-sus is waiting to save you!
An-gels are longing to tell the glad news, Je-sus is waiting to save you!
Why turn a-way, and to Je-sus say "No?" Je-sus is waiting to save you!
Par-don is purchased, salva-tion is free; Je-sus is waiting to save you!
Come to Him now, not a moment de-lay; Je-sus is waiting to save you!
    save you now!

CHORUS.

Come to Him now, come to Him now, Je-sus is waiting to save you!
    save you now!

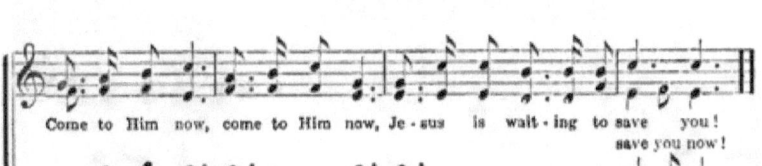

Come to Him now, come to Him now, Je-sus is wait-ing to save you!
    save you now!

74. The Loving Shepherd.

"I am the good Shepherd: the good Shepherd giveth His life for the sheep."—*John* 10:11.

W. A. OGDEN. W. A. OGDEN.

1. Je-sus, the lov-ing Shepherd, Call-eth thee now to come
 In-to the fold of safe-ty, Where there is rest and room.
 Come in the strength of man-hood, Come in the morn of youth,
 En-ter the fold of safe-ty, En-ter the way of truth.

2. Je-sus, the lov-ing Shepherd, Gave His dear life for thee,
 Ten-der-ly now He's call-ing, Wan-der-er, come to Me.
 Haste, for with-out is dan-ger, Come, cries the Shep-herd blest,
 En-ter the fold of safe-ty, En-ter the place of rest.

3. Lin-ger-ing is but fol-ly, Wolves are a-broad to-day,
 Seeking the sheep who're straying, Seek-ing the lambs to slay.
 Je-sus, the lov-ing Shepherd, Call-eth thee now to come
 In-to the fold of safe-ty, Where there is rest and room.

CHORUS *Arranged.*

Lovingly, tenderly, calling is He; Wanderer, wanderer, come unto Me.

From "*Gathered Jewels*," by permission. Copyright.

The Loving Shepherd—*Concluded.*

Patiently waiting, there standing I see Jesus my Shepherd di - vine.

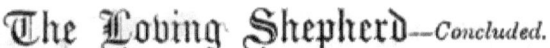

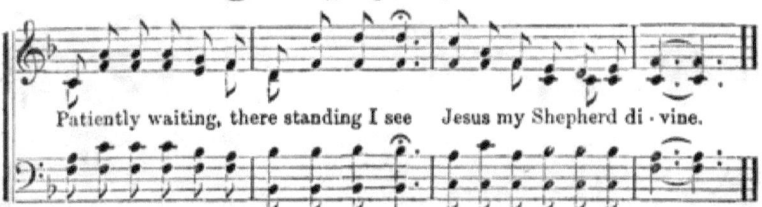

75 Just Now Believe.

R. Kelso Carter. John R. Sweney.

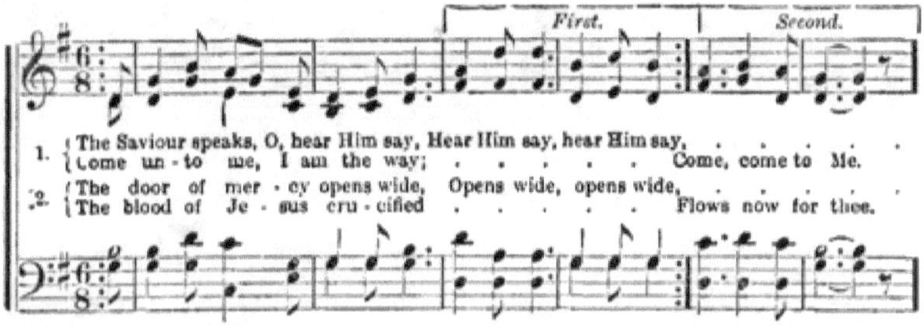
First.
Second.
1. The Saviour speaks, O, hear Him say, Hear Him say, hear Him say,
Come un - to me, I am the way; Come, come to Me.
2. The door of mer - cy opens wide, Opens wide, opens wide,
The blood of Je - sus cru - cified Flows now for thee.

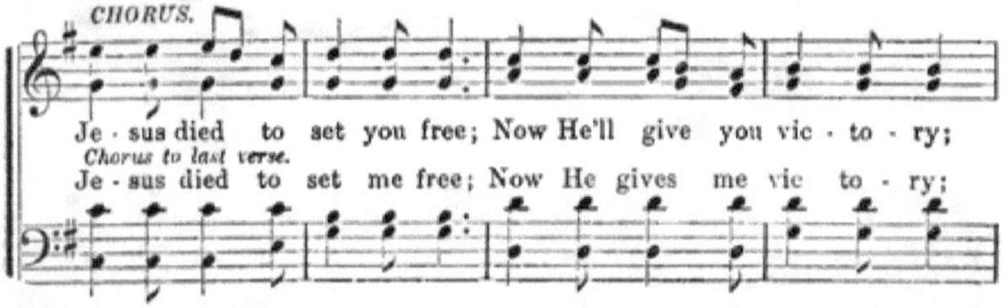
CHORUS.
Je - sus died to set you free; Now He'll give you vic - to - ry;
Chorus to last verse.
Je - sus died to set me free; Now He gives me vic to - ry;

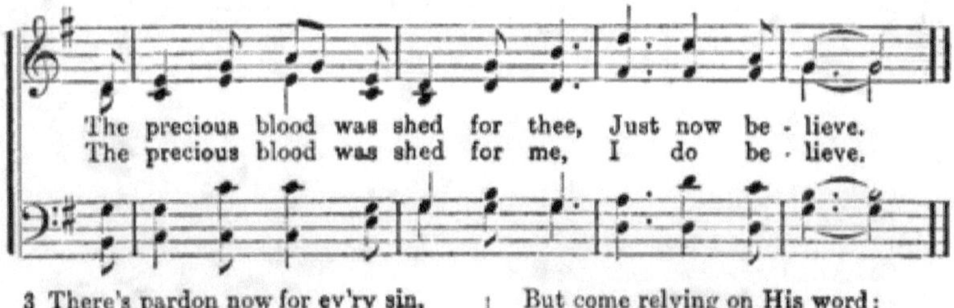
The precious blood was shed for thee, Just now be - lieve.
The precious blood was shed for me, I do be - lieve.

3 There's pardon now for ev'ry sin,
Every sin, every sin,
And perfect purity within;
Come and be free.

4 O, do not fear to trust the Lord,
Trust the Lord, trust the Lord,
But come relying on His word;
Christ died for thee.

5 The life of faith is wondrous sweet,
Wondrous sweet, wondrous sweet,
To daily sit at Jesus feet;
Come, come and see.

From "*Songs of Perfect Love*," by permission. Copyright.

76. Hark, the Voice of Jesus Calling!

M. B. Sleight. H. R. Palmer, by per.

1. Hark! the voice of Jesus calling, "Follow Me, follow Me!"

Softly thro' the silence falling, "Follow, follow Me!"

As of old He called the fishers, When He walked by Galilee,

rit.

Still His patient voice is pleading, "Follow, follow Me!"

2 Who will heed the holy mandate,
  "Follow Me, follow Me!"
Leaving all things at His bidding,
  "Follow, follow Me!"
Hark! that tender voice entreating
Mariners on life's rough sea,
Gently, lovingly repeating,
  "Follow, follow Me!"

3 Harken, lest He plead no longer,
  "Follow Me, follow Me!"
Once again, O hear Him calling,
  "Follow, follow Me!"
Turning swift at Thy sweet summons,
Evermore, O Christ, would we,
For Thy love all else forsaking,
Follow, follow Thee.

77. The Gospel Ship.

Old Melody.

1 The Gospel Ship along is sailing,
   Bound for Canaan's peaceful shore;
 All who wish to sail to glory,
   Come and welcome, rich and poor.

CHORUS.
"Glory, glory, hallelujah!" all the
   sailors loudly cry,
"See the blissful port of glory, open
   to each faithful eye!"

2 Millions now are safely landed
   Over on the golden shore;
 Millions more are on their journey,
   Yet there's room for millions more.

3 Come on board, and ship for glory;
   Be in haste, make up your mind,
 For our vessel's weighing anchor,
   You will soon be left behind.

4 Do not fear the ship will founder,
   Though the foaming billows roar,
 Jesus Christ will safely guide her
   To her destined happy shore.

5 You have kindred over yonder,
   On that bright and happy shore;
 By and by we'll swell the number,
   When the toils of life are o'er

78. The Blessed Feast.

Fanny J. Crosby. "Come, for all things are now ready."—Luke 14: 17. W. H. Doane.

1. Come, poor sinner, to the blessed, blessed feast, O hear the call—thy Saviour's call;
Haste to meet Him, He will welcome thee His guest,
O rejoice, there's room for all.
D. C.—Come to Jesus, He is waiting, waiting now;
Come, O come, there's room for all.

REFRAIN.
Whosoever will in that feast may share, In our Father's house there is bread to spare:

2 Art thou weary, would'st thou lay thy weight aside? [near,
Then rest thee here, the cross is near,
See where Jesus, thy Redeemer, bled and died;
Come and taste His mercy here.

3 Come to Jesus, and thy burden He will bear;
The feast is spread, lift up thy head;
Come and rest thee in the Saviour's gentle care,
By His love thou shalt be fed.

79. The Gospel Invitation.

J. Hart. Tune: No. 95.

1 Come, ye sinners, poor and needy,
Weak and wounded, sick and sore:
Jesus ready stands to save you,
Full of pity, love and power:
‖: He is able,
He is willing; doubt no more. :‖

2 Now, ye needy, come, and welcome;
God's free bounty glorify;
True belief, and true repentance,—
Every grace that brings you nigh.
‖: Without money,
Come to Jesus Christ, and buy. :‖

3 Let not conscience make you linger,
Nor of fitness fondly dream:
All the fitness He requireth
Is to feel your need of Him:
‖: This He gives you,—
'Tis the Spirit's glimmering beam. :‖

4 Come, ye weary, heavy-laden,
Bruised and mangled by the fall
If you tarry till you're better
You will never come at all;
‖: Not the righteous,—
Sinners Jesus came to call. :‖

80. More to Follow.

P. P. Bliss. Key of E. (G. H. 32.)

1 Have you on the Lord believed?
Still there's more to follow;
Of His grace have you received?
Still there's more to follow,
Oh, the grace the Father shows!
Still there's more to follow;
Freely He His grace bestows,
Still there's more to follow.

Cho—More and more, more and more,
Always more to follow;
Oh, His matchless, boundless love!
Still there's more to follow.

2 Have you felt the Saviour near?
Still there's more to follow;
Does His blessed presence cheer?
Still there's more to follow.
Oh! the love that Jesus shows!
Still there's more to follow;
Freely He His love bestows,
Still there's more to follow.

3 Have you felt the Spirit's power?
Still there's more to follow:
Falling like the gentle shower,
Still there's more to follow:
Oh, the power the Spirit shows,
Still there's more to follow:
Freely He His power bestows,
Still there's more to follow.

81. Art Thou Lost?

W. F. S. Arranged.
Impressively.
W. F. Sherwin.

1. Art thou lost, lost, lost! Wandering one, wail-ing a-lone? In the dark, dark, past, Beameth no light for thee? Lo! a strong hand thro' the darkness doth move: Lo! a sweet voice bears this message of love: "I the blest Je-sus came down from a-bove, To seek and to save the lost!"

2. O, believe on Him, Sorrowing one, faint-ing a-lone; To the Sav-iour cling, Trusting His simple word. On-ly believe He is a-ble to do All that you ask, or is needed by you; Je-sus is ready your soul to re-new; Then just as you are, O come!

3. O be saved, saved, saved! Perishing one, trembling a-lone; In thy Fa-ther's house, Man-y wait thy re-turn. Rise, like the prodigal, haste to thy home! Flee from the shadows of gathering gloom! Angels now waiting will help thee to come; And heaven will ring with joy!

By permission.   Copyright.

82. All for Jesus.

Mrs. Mary D. James. Mrs. Joseph F. Knapp.

1. All for Jesus! all for Jesus! All my being's ransomed powers;
2. Let my hands perform His bidding. Let my feet run in His ways,—
3. Since my eyes were fixed on Jesus, I've lost sight of all beside;
4. Oh, what wonder! how amazing! Jesus—glorious King of kings—

All my thoughts, and words, and doings, All my days, and all my hours.
Let my eyes see Jesus only, Let my lips speak forth His praise.
So enchained my spirit's vision, Looking at the Crucified!
Deigns to call me His beloved, Lets me rest beneath His wings!

CHORUS.

All for Jesus! all for Jesus! All my days, and all my hours.
All for Jesus! all for Jesus! Let my lips speak forth His praise.
All for Jesus! all for Jesus! All for Jesus Crucified!
All for Jesus! all for Jesus! Resting now beneath His wings!

All for Jesus! all for Jesus! All my days, and all my hours.
All for Jesus! all for Jesus! Let my lips speak forth His praise.
All for Jesus! all for Jesus! All for Jesus Crucified!
All for Jesus! all for Jesus! Resting now beneath His wings!

By permission. Copyright.

83. Take Me as I Am.

(Use No. 101 with this Tune and Chorus.)

J. H. S. Arranged.   Ch'd and Arr. by H. T. C. & W. J. B.

1. Je-sus, my Lord, to Thee I cry, Un-less Thou help me I must die;
2. Helpless I am and full of guilt, But yet for me Thy blood was spilt.
3. No pre-pa-ra-tion can I make, My best resolves I on-ly break.
4. I thirst, I long to know Thy love, Thy full sal-va-tion I would prove;
5. Spir-it of God, now breathe on me, The Saviour's glo-ry make me see;

Oh, bring Thy free sal-va-tion nigh, And take me as I am.
And Thou can'st make me what Thou wilt, But take me as I am.
Yet save me for Thine own name's sake, And take me as I am.
And now to Thee my soul does move, Oh, take me as I am.
Changed to His im-age let me be; Come take me as I am.

D.S.—Oh, bring Thy free sal-va-tion nigh, And take me as I am.
He brings His free sal-va-tion nigh, And takes me as I am.

CHORUS.

Now take me as I am, Now take me as I am;
2nd chorus.
He takes me as I am, He takes me as I am;

84. I Can, I Will, I Do Believe.

(Use Nos. 78 and 101 with this Chorus.)

I can, I will, I do be-lieve, I can, I will, I do believe,
I can, I will, I do be-lieve That Je-sus . . . saves me now.

1 Just as I am, without one plea,
But that Thy blood was shed for me,
And that Thou bidd'st me come to Thee,
O Lamb of God, I come.

2 Just as I am, Thou dost receive,
Dost welcome, pardon, cleanse, relieve,
Because Thy promise I believe,
O Lamb of God, I come.

90. Nearer, My God, to Thee.

S. F. Adams.   Lowell Mason.

1. Near-er, my God, to Thee, Near-er to Thee; E'en tho' it be a cross That rais-eth me; Still all my song shall be, Near-er, my God, to Thee, Nearer, my God, to Thee, Near-er to Thee.

2 There let the way appear,
   Steps unto heaven;
All that Thou sendest me,
   In mercy given;
Angels to beckon me
|: Nearer, my God, to Thee, :|
   Nearer to Thee.

3 Or if on joyful wing,
   Cleaving the sky,
Sun, moon, and stars forgot,
   Upward I fly,
Still all my song shall be,
|: Nearer, my God, to Thee, :|
   Nearer to Thee.

91. More Love to Thee.

Mrs. Prentiss.   Tune: No. 90.

1 More love to Thee, O Christ!
   More love to Thee;
Hear Thou the prayer I make
   On bended knee;
This is my earnest plea,
|: More love, O Christ, to Thee, :|
   More love to Thee!

2 Once earthly joy I craved,
   Sought peace and rest;
Now Thee alone I seek,
   Give what is best;

This all my prayer shall be,
|: More love, O Christ, to Thee, :|
   More love to Thee!

3 Then shall my latest breath,
   Whisper Thy praise,
This be the parting cry
   My heart shall raise;
This still its prayer shall be,
|: More love, O Christ, to Thee, :|
   More love to Thee!

92. Working with Thee.

Tune: No. 90.

1 Working, O Christ, with Thee
   Working with Thee,
Unworthy, sinful, weak,
   Though we may be,
Our all to Thee we give,
For Thee alone would live,
And by Thy grace achieve,
   Working with Thee.

2 Saviour, we weary not
   Working with Thee;
As hard as Thine our lot
   Can never be;

Our joy and comfort this,
"Thy grace sufficient is,"
This changes toil to bliss,
   Working with Thee.

3 So let us labor on,
   Working with Thee,
Till earth to Thee is won,
   From sin set free,
Till man, from shore to shore,
Receive Thee and adore,
And join us evermore,
   Working with Thee.

95 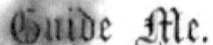 Guide Me.

W. WILLIAMS. Changed by H. T. C.

2 Open now the crystal fountain,
   Whence the healing streams do flow;
   Let the fiery, cloudy pillar
   Lead me all my journey through:
   ||:Strong Deliverer,
   Be Thou still my strength and shield.:||

3 When I tread the verge of Jordan,
   Bid its waters then divide;
   Bear me through in faith triumphant,
   Land me safe on Canaan's side:
   ||:Songs of praises,
   I will ever give to Thee.:||

96 Come, Thou Fount.

ROBINSON. Changed by H. T. C.   TUNE: "Guide Me," No. 95.

1 Come, Thou Fount of every blessing,
   Tune my heart to sing Thy grace,
   Streams of mercy, never ceasing,
   Call for songs of loudest praise.

   CHORUS.
   I love Jesus, Hallelujah!
   I love Jesus, yes I do;
   I love Jesus, He's my Saviour,
   Jesus smiles and loves me too.

2 Jesus sought me when a stranger,
   Wandering from the fold of God;
   He to rescue me from danger,
   Interposed His precious blood.

3 O to grace how great a debtor
   Daily I'm constrained to be!
   Let Thy goodness, like a fetter,
   Bind my trusting heart to Thee.

4 I do trust Thee, Lord, I know it;
   I will trust, for Thou art love;
   Here's my heart, O take and seal it,
   Seal it for Thy courts above!

97 Parting Hymn.

REV. W. SHIRLEY.   TUNE: "Guide Me," No. 95.

1 Lord, dismiss us with Thy blessing,
   Fill our heart with joy and peace;
   Let us each Thy love possessing,
   Triumph in redeeming grace;
   O refresh us,
   Travelling through this wilderness.

2 Thanks we give, and adoration,
   For Thy gospel's joyful sound;
   May the fruits of Thy salvation
   In our hearts and lives abound;
   May Thy presence
   With us evermore be found.

3 So, whene'er the signal's given,
   Us from earth to call away,
   Borne on angels' wings to heaven,
   Glad the summons to obey,
   May we ever
   Reign with Christ in endless day.

98. What a Friend.

Dr. Bonar. C. C. Converse.

1. What a Friend we have in Je-sus, All our sins and griefs to bear!
What a priv-i-lege to car-ry Ev-'ry-thing to God in prayer!
D.S.—All be-cause we do not car-ry Ev-'ry-thing to God in prayer!
O what peace we of-ten for-feit, O what needless pain we bear,

2 Have we trials and temptations?
Is there trouble anywhere?
We should never be discouraged,
Take it to the Lord in prayer.
Can we find a friend so faithful,
Who will all our sorrows share?
Jesus knows our every weakness,
Take it to the Lord in prayer.

3 Are we weak and heavy laden,
Cumbered with a load of care?—
Precious Saviour, still our refuge—
Take it to the Lord in prayer.
Do thy friends despise, forsake thee?
Take it to the Lord in prayer;
In His arms He'll take and shield thee,
Thou wilt find a solace there.

99. Love Divine.

C. Wesley. Tune: No. 98.

1 Love Divine, all love excelling,
 Joy of Heaven to earth come down;
Fix in us Thy humble dwelling,
 All Thy faithful mercies crown;
Jesus, Thou art all compassion,
 Pure, unbounded love Thou art;
Visit us with Thy salvation,
 Enter every trembling heart.

2 Breathe, O breathe Thy loving Spirit
 Into every troubled breast;
Let us all in Thee inherit,
 Let us find Thy promised rest.

Come, Almighty to deliver,
 Let us all Thy grace receive
Suddenly return, and never,
 Nevermore Thy temples leave!

3 Finish then Thy new creation,
 Pure and spotless let us be;
Let us see Thy great salvation,
 Perfectly restored in Thee.
Changed from glory into glory,
 Till in heaven we take our place;
Till we cast our crowns before Thee,
 Lost in wonder, love, and praise.

100. Saviour, Like a Shepherd.

D. A. Thrupp. Tune: No. 98.

1 Saviour, like a shepherd lead us,
 Much we need Thy tend'rest care,
In Thy pleasant pastures feed us,
 For our use Thy folds prepare;
[:Blessed Jesus, blessed Jesus,
 Thou hast bought us, Thine we are.:]

2 We are Thine, do Thou befriend us,
 Be the Guardian of our way;
Keep Thy flock, from sin defend us,
 Seek us when we go astray;
[:Blessed Jesus, blessed Jesus,
 Hear, O hear us, when we pray.:]

3 Early let us seek Thy favor,
 Early let us do Thy will;
Blessed Lord, and only Saviour,
 With Thy love our bosoms fill:
[:Blessed Jesus, blessed Jesus,
 Thou hast loved us, love us still.:]

101. Just as I Am.

"Him that cometh to Me, I will in no wise cast out."—John 6: 37.

MISS CHARLOTTE ELLIOTT. WM. D. BRADBURY.

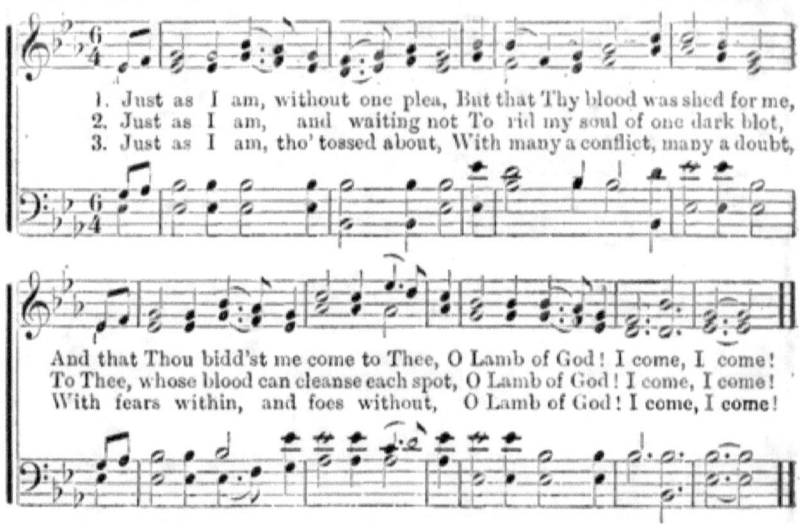

1. Just as I am, without one plea, But that Thy blood was shed for me,
2. Just as I am, and waiting not To rid my soul of one dark blot,
3. Just as I am, tho' tossed about, With many a conflict, many a doubt,

And that Thou bidd'st me come to Thee, O Lamb of God! I come, I come!
To Thee, whose blood can cleanse each spot, O Lamb of God! I come, I come!
With fears within, and foes without, O Lamb of God! I come, I come!

4 Just as I am; Thou wilt receive,
  Wilt welcome, pardon, cleanse, relieve;
  Because Thy promise I believe,
    O Lamb of God! I come, I come!

5 Just as I am—Thy love unknown
  Has broken every barrier down;
  Now to be Thine, yea, Thine alone,
    O Lamb of God! I come, I come!

102. Ashamed of Jesus.

REV. JOSEPH GRIGG. TUNE: No. 101.

1 Jesus, and shall it ever be,
  A mortal man ashamed of Thee?
  Ashamed of Thee whom angels praise,
  Whose glories shine thro' endless days?

2 Ashamed of Jesus, that dear Friend
  On whom my hopes of heaven depend?
  No, when I blush, be this my shame,
  That I no more revere His name.

3 Ashamed of Jesus! Yes, I may,
  When I've no guilt to wash away,
  No tear to wipe, no good to crave,
  No fear to quell, no soul to save.

4 Till then, nor is my boasting vain,
  Till then I boast a Saviour slain;
  And O, may this my glory be,
  That Christ is not ashamed of me.

103. The Mercy-Seat.

REV. H. STOWELL. TUNE: No. 101.

1 From every stormy wind that blows,
  From every swelling tide of woes,
  There is a calm, a sure retreat;
  'Tis found beneath the mercy-seat.

2 There is a place where Jesus sheds
  The oil of gladness on our heads;
  A place than all besides more sweet;
  It is the blood-bought mercy-seat.

3 There is a place where spirits blend,
  Where friend holds fellowship with friend;
  Though sundered far, by faith they meet
  Around one common mercy-seat.

4 Ah! whither could we flee for aid,
  When tempted, desolate, dismayed?
  Or how the hosts of hell defeat,
  Had suffering saints no mercy-seat?

104 My Heart's Desire.

C. WESLEY   TUNE: No. 101.

1 O Thou who camest from above
    The pure celestial fire to impart,
  Kindle a flame of sacred love
    On the mean altar of my heart.

2 There let it for Thy glory burn
    With inextinguishable blaze,
  And trembling to its source return
    In humble prayer and fervent
      praise.

3 Jesus, confirm my heart's desire
    To work, and speak, and think for
      Thee;
  Still let me guard the holy fire,
    And still stir up Thy gift in me.

4 Ready for all Thy perfect will,
    My acts of faith and love repeat,
  Till death Thy endless mercies seal,
    And make the sacrifice complete.

105 Near the Cross.

F. J. CROSBY.   (G. H. 45.)

1 Jesus, keep me near the cross,
    There a precious fountain,
    Free to all, a healing stream—
      Flows from Calvary's mountain

CHORUS.

In the cross, in the cross,
  Be my glory ever;
Till my raptured soul shal' find
  Rest beyond the river.

2 Near the cross, a trembling soul,
    Love and mercy found me;
  There the bright and morning star
    Shed its beams around me.

3 Near the cross, O Lamb of God!
    Bring its scenes before me;
  Help me walk from day to day,
    With its shadows o'er me.

4 Near the cross I'll watch and wait,
    Hoping, trusting ever,
  Till I reach the golden strand,
    Just beyond the river.

106 Every Day and Hour.

F. J. CROSBY.   (G. H. 43.)

1 Saviour, more than life to me,
  I am clinging, clinging close to Thee!
  Let Thy precious blood applied,
  Keep me ever, ever near Thy side.

CHORUS.

Every day, every hour,
Let me feel Thy cleansing power;
May Thy tender love to me
Bind me closer, closer, Lord, to Thee.

2 Through this changing world below,
  Lead me gently, gently as I go;
  Trusting Thee, I cannot stray,
  I can never, never lose my way.

3 Let me love Thee more and more,
  Till this fleeting, fleeting life is o'er;
  Till my soul is lost in love
  In a brighter, brighter world above.

107 Pass Me Not.

F. J. CROSBY.   (G. H. 27.)

1 Pass me not, O gentle Saviour,
    Hear my humble cry;
  While on others Thou art smiling,
    Do not pass me by.

CHORUS.

Saviour, Saviour, hear my humble
    cry;
While on others Thou art calling,
    Do not pass me by.

2 Let me at a throne of mercy
    Find a sweet relief,
  Kneeling there in deep contrition,
    Help my unbelief.

3 Trusting only in Thy merit,
    Would I seek Thy face;
  Heal my wounded, broken spirit,
    Save me by Thy grace.

4 Thou the Spring of all my comfort,
    More than life to me,
  Whom have I on earth beside Thee?
    Whom in heaven but Thee?

108. I Do Believe.

E. P. HAMMOND. — OLD MELODY.

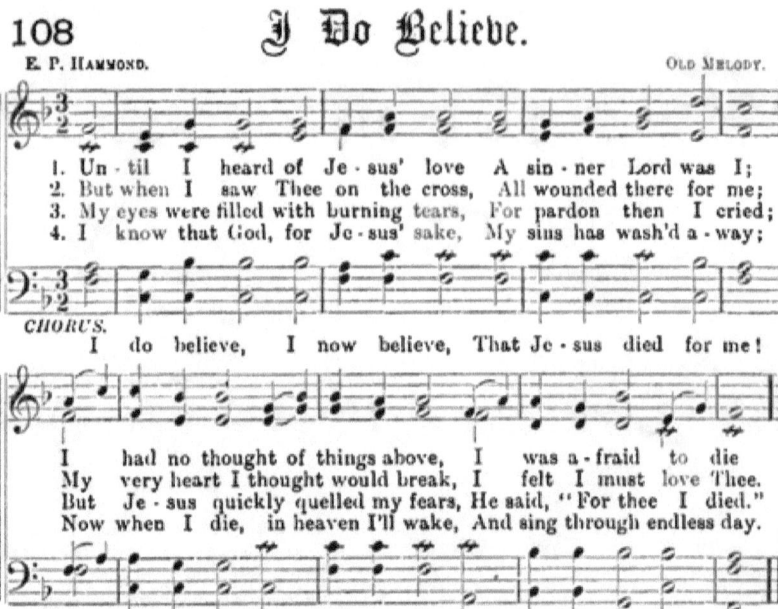

1. Un-til I heard of Je-sus' love A sin-ner Lord was I;
2. But when I saw Thee on the cross, All wounded there for me;
3. My eyes were filled with burning tears, For pardon then I cried;
4. I know that God, for Je-sus' sake, My sins has wash'd a-way;

CHORUS.
I do believe, I now believe, That Je-sus died for me!

I had no thought of things above, I was a-fraid to die
My very heart I thought would break, I felt I must love Thee.
But Je-sus quickly quelled my fears, He said, "For thee I died."
Now when I die, in heaven I'll wake, And sing through endless day.

And thro' His blood—His precious blood—I shall from sin be free!

109. All-Victorious Love.

I. WATTS. — TUNE: No. 108.

1 Jesus, Thine all victorious love,
  Shed in my heart abroad:
  Then shall my feet no longer rove,
  Rooted and fixed in God.

  CHORUS.
  I can believe, I now believe,
  That Jesus died for me;
  A token of His love He gives,
  A pledge of liberty.

2 O that in me the sacred fire
  Might now begin to glow,
  Burn up the dross of base desire,
  And make the mountains flow.

3 Refining fire go through my heart,
  Illuminate my soul;
  Scatter Thy life through every part,
  And sanctify the whole.

4 My steadfast soul, from falling free,
  Shall then no longer move;
  But Christ be all the world to me.
  And all my heart be love.

110. The Name of Jesus.

J. NEWTON. — TUNE: No. 108.

1 How sweet the name of Jesus sounds
  In a believer's ear;
  It soothes his sorrows, heals his wounds,
  And drives away His fear.

  CHORUS.
  I do believe, I now believe,
  That Jesus died for me;
  That on the cross He shed His blood
  From sin to set me free.

2 It makes the wounded spirit whole,
  And calms the troubled breast·

'Tis manna to the hungry soul,
And to the weary rest.

3 Dear Name! the Rock on which I build,
  My shield and hiding-place;
  My never-failing treasury, filled
  With boundless stores of grace.

4 Jesus! my Saviour, Shepherd, Friend,
  My Prophet, Priest, and King,
  My Lord, My Life, my Way, my End;
  Accept the praise I bring.

111 A Charge to Keep.
C. WESLEY.   (G. H. 113.)

1 A charge to keep I have,
  A God to glorify,
  A never dying soul to save,
  And fit it for the sky.

2 To serve the present age,
  My calling to fulfil,
  O may it all my powers engage,
  To do my Master's will.

3 Arm me with jealous care,
  As in Thy sight to live;
  And O, Thy servant, Lord, prepare,
  A strict account to give.

4 Help me to watch and pray,
  And on Thyself rely;
  Assured, if I my trust betray,
  I must forever die.

112 Sing of His Mighty Love.
DR. BOTTOME.   (G. H. 46.)

1 Oh, bliss of the purified, bliss of the free,   [for me;
  I plunge in the crimson tide opened
  O'er sin and uncleanness exulting I stand,
  And point to the print of the nails in His hand.

CHORUS.
Oh, sing of His mighty love,
‖:Sing of His mighty love,:‖
Mighty to save.

2 Oh, bliss of the purified, Jesus is mine,
  No longer in dread condemnation I pine;   [grace,
  In conscious salvation I sing of His
  Who lifteth upon me the light of His face.

3 Oh, bliss of the purified, bliss of the pure,
  No wound hath the soul that His blood cannot cure;
  No sorrow-bowed head but may sweetly find rest,   [breast.
  No tears but may dry them on Jesus'

4 O Jesus the crucified, Thee will I sing,
  My blessed Redeemer, my God and my King;
  My soul filled with rapture shall shout o'er the grave,   [to Save."
  And triumph in death in the "Mighty

113 Lord, I Hear.
ELIZABETH CODNER.   (G. H. 87.)

1 Lord, I hear of showers of blessing
  Thou art scattering, full and free—
  Showers, the thirsty land refreshing:
  Let some droppings fall on me—
    Even me, even me, etc.

2 Pass me not, O gracious Father,
  Sinful tho' my heart may be;
  Thou might'st leave me, but the rather
  Let Thy mercy fall on me—
    Even me, even me, etc.

3 Pass me not, O tender Saviour!
  Let me love and cling to Thee;
  I am longing for Thy favor;
  Whilst Thou'rt calling, oh, call me—
    Even me, even me, etc.

4 Pass me not, O mighty Spirit!
  Thou canst make the blind to see;
  Witnesser of Jesus' merit,
  Speak the word of power to me—
    Even me, even me, etc.

5 Pass me not! Thy lost one bringing,
  Bind my heart, O Lord, to Thee;
  While the streams of life are springing,
  Blessing others, oh, bless me—
    Even me, even me, etc.

114 I Need Thee Every Hour.
MRS. ANNIE S. HAWKS.   (G. H. 3.)

1 I need Thee every hour,
  Most gracious Lord:
  No tender voice like Thine
  Can peace afford.

CHORUS.
I need Thee, oh, I need Thee;
Every hour I need Thee;
Oh, bless me now, my Saviour
I come to Thee.

2 I need Thee every hour;
  Stay Thou near by:
  Temptations lose their power
  When Thou art nigh.

3 I need Thee every hour,
  Teach me Thy will;
  And Thy rich promises
  In me fulfil.

4 I need Thee every hour,
  Most Holy One;
  Oh, make me Thine indeed,
  Thou blessed Son.

115. I Will, I Do Believe.

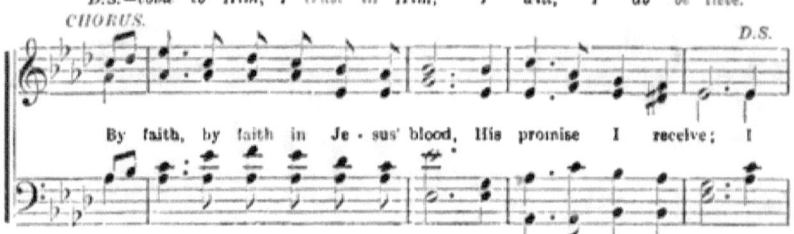

1. Come, O my God, the promise seal, This mountain sin re-move;
   Now in my waiting soul re-veal The vir-tue of Thy love.
2. Let an-ger, sloth, de-sire and pride, This mo-ment be sub-dued;
   Be cast in-to the crimson tide Of my Redeem-er's blood.

D.S.—come to Him, I trust in Him, I will, I do be-lieve.

CHORUS.

By faith, by faith in Je-sus' blood, His promise I receive; I

3 Saviour, to Thee my soul looks up,
  My present Saviour Thou!
  In all the confidence of hope,
  I claim the blessing now.

'Tis done; Thou dost this moment save,
  With full salvation bless;
  Redemption through Thy blood I have,
  And spotless love and peace.

116 O For a Heart to Praise My God.

C. Wesley. TUNE: No. 115.

1 O for a heart to praise my God,
  A heart from sin set free!
  A heart that always feels Thy blood
  So freely spilt for me!

CHORUS.
By faith, by faith in Jesus' blood,
  His promise I receive;
  I come to Him, I trust in Him,
  I will, I do believe.

2 A heart resigned, submissive, meek,
  My great Redeemer's throne;
  Where only Christ is heard to speak,
  Where Jesus reigns alone.

3 A humble, lowly, contrite heart,
  Believing, true, and clean;
  Which neither life nor death can part
  From Him that dwells within.

4 A heart in every thought renewed,
  And full of love divine;
  Perfect, and right, and pure, and good,
  A copy, Lord, of Thine.

5 Thy nature, gracious Lord, impart;
  Come quickly from above;
  Write Thy new name upon my heart,
  Thy new, best name of love.

117 Abide with Me.

Rev. H. F. Lyte. TUNE: D. H. 237. KEY OF E FLAT.

Abide with me, fast falls the eventide;
The darkness deepens; Lord, with me abide!
When other helpers fail, and comforts flee,
Help of the helpless, O abide with me!

2 Swift to its close ebbs out life's little day,
  Earth's joys grow dim, its glories pass away;
  Change and decay in all around I see;
  O Thou who changest not, abide with me!

3 I need Thy presence every passing hour;
  What but Thy grace can foil the tempter's power?

Who like Thyself my guide and stay can be?
Through cloud and sunshine, O abide with me!

4 I fear no foe with Thee at hand to bless;
  Ills have no weight, and tears no bitterness;
  Where is death's sting? where, grave, thy vic-
  I triumph still, if Thou abide with me. [tory?

5 Reveal Thyself before my closing eyes;
  Shine through the gloom, and point me to the
  skies;   [shadows flee;
  Heaven's morning breaks, and earth's vain
  In life and death, O Lord, abide with me!

118. Pentecostal Power.

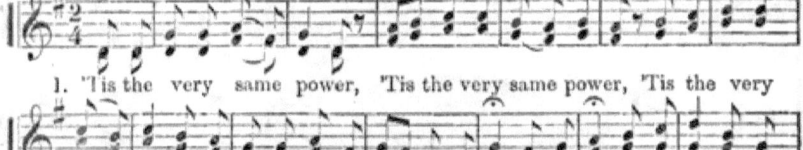

OLD MELODY. Arranged.

1. 'Tis the very same power, 'Tis the very same power, 'Tis the very same power they had at Pentecost; 'Tis the power, 'Tis the power, 'Tis the power [Jesus promised should come down. Send it now, send it now, Send the power Jesus [promised should come down.

2 While with one accord assembled,
All in an upper room,
Came the power, etc., Send it now, etc.

3 'Twas while they all were praying,
And believing it would come,
Came the power, etc., Send it now, etc.

4 Three thousand were converted
And added to the Church,
By the power, etc., Send it now, etc.

5 Our fathers had this power,
And we may have it, too;
Send the power, etc., Send it now, etc.

6 'Tis the very same power,
For I feel it in my soul;
'Tis the power, etc., Send it now, etc.

119. Holy Spirit, Faithful Guide.

M. M. WELLS.   TUNE: G. H. 40.   KEY G.

1 Holy Spirit, faithful Guide,
Ever near the Christian's side;
Gently lead us by the hand,
Pilgrims in a desert land;
Weary souls for e'er rejoice,
While they hear that sweetest voice,
Whispering softly, Wanderer, come!
Follow Me, I'll guide thee home.

2 Ever present, truest friend,
Ever near, Thine aid to lend,
Leave us not to doubt and fear,
Groping on in darkness drear;
When the storms are raging sore,
Hearts grow faint and hopes give o'er,
Whispering softly, Wanderer, come!
Follow Me, I'll guide thee home.

120. Lord's Prayer.

Our Father, which art in heaven, hallowed . . . be Thy name; Thy kingdom come, Thy will be done on . . . earth as it is in heaven. Give us this day our . . . dai-ly bread; And forgive us our tres- passes, as we forgive those who trespass against us And lead us not into tempta- tion, but deliver . . . us from evil, For Thine is the kingdom, and the power, and the glory, forever. Amen.

121. Martyn.

C. Wesley. — Simeon Butler Marsh.

1 Jesus, Lover of my soul,
  Let me to Thy bosom fly,
While the nearer waters roll,
  While the tempest still is high.
Hide me, oh, my Saviour, hide,
  Till the storm of life be past;
Safe into the haven guide,
  Oh, receive my soul at last.

2 Other refuge have I none,
  Hangs my helpless soul on Thee
Leave, ah, leave me not alone,
  Still support and comfort me.

All my trust on Thee is stayed,
  All my help from Thee I bring;
Cover my defenceless head
  With the shadow of Thy wing.

3 Plenteous grace with Thee is found—
  Grace to cover all my sin;
Let the healing streams abound;
  Make and keep me pure within.
Thou of life the Fountain art,
  Freely let me take of Thee:
Spring Thou up within my heart;
  Rise to all eternity.

122. Consecration Prayer.

Miss Havergal. — Ignace Pleyel.

1 Take my life and let it be
  Consecrated, Lord, to Thee;
Take my moments and my days,
  Let them flow in ceaseless praise.

2 Take my hands and let them move
  At the impulse of Thy love;
Take my feet and let them be
  Swift and beautiful for Thee.

3 Take my silver and my gold—
  Not a mite would I withhold;
Take my intellect and use
  Every power as Thou shalt choose.

4 Take my voice and let me sing
  Always, only, for my King;
Take my lips and let them be
  Filled with messages from Thee.

5 Take my will and make it Thine,
  It shall be no longer mine;
Take my heart, it is Thine own;
  It shall be Thy royal throne.

6 Take my love, my Lord, I pour
  At Thy feet its treasure store;
Take myself, and I will be,
  Ever, only, all for Thee.

123. Gloria Patri.

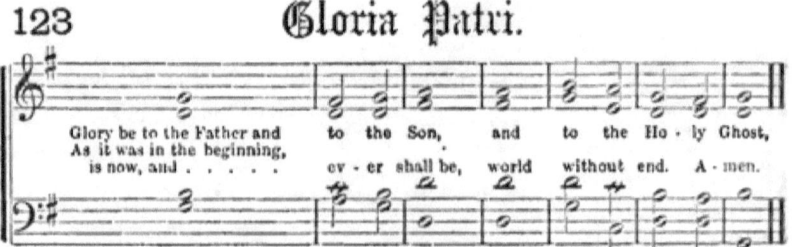

Glory be to the Father and to the Son, and to the Ho-ly Ghost,
As it was in the beginning, is now, and . . . . . ev-er shall be, world without end. A-men.

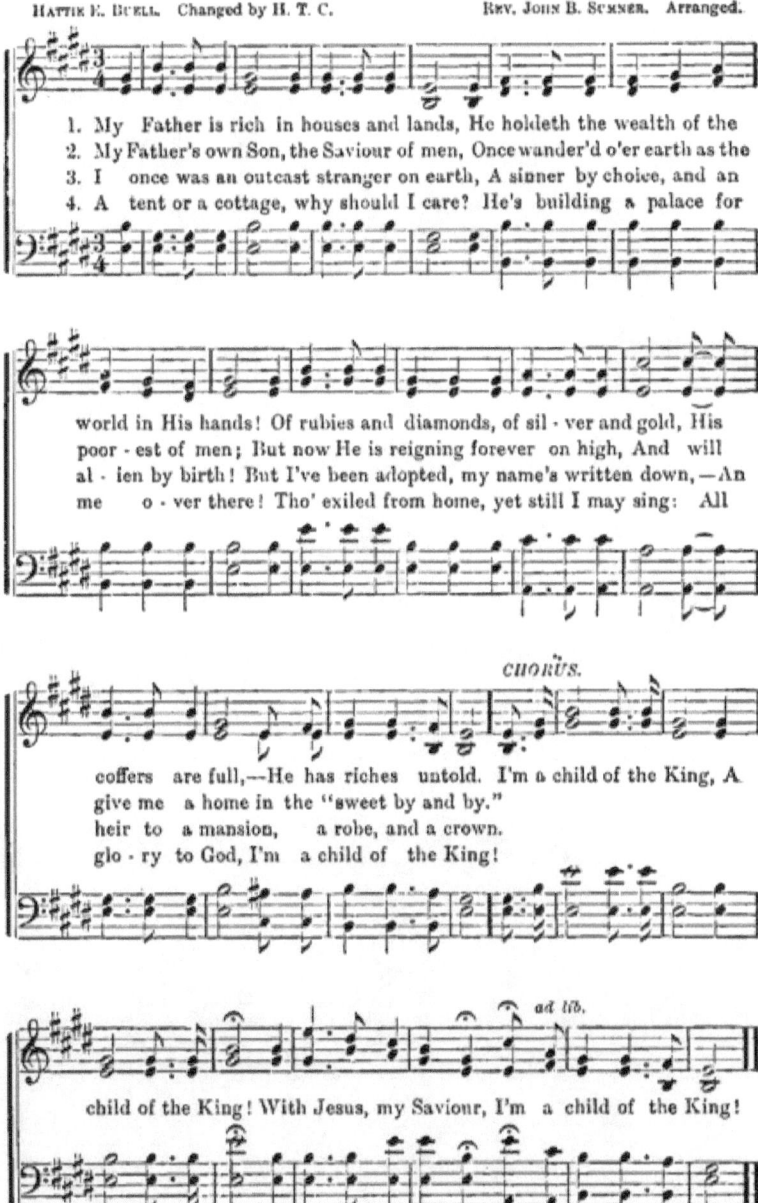

Believing and Receiving—Concluded.

trusting in the Lord, For the blood of Jesus cleanseth me.
cleanseth me.

128. Safe in Thy Arms.

Geo. Cooper. H. Millard. Arranged.

1. Safe in Thy arms, O Saviour dear and blest! How sure the
2. Safe in Thy arms, Thy loving smile shall be My sunlight,
3. Safe in Thy arms, dear balm for earthly woe! Joy of my
4. Safe in Thy arms, Oh, joyful thought each hour! Oh, blissful

refuge, sweet the perfect rest! No ills that meet us here, no storms, no
Jesus, thro' e-ter-ni-ty! No other hope have I, no other
pathway while I plod below! Die far away the storms that round me
haven when earth-tempests lower! Still onward guide us, Saviour kind and

care, O Saviour mine, can ev-er find us there!
stay, O Saviour, lead me nearer ev - - 'ry day!
beat, O Saviour mine, whilst Thou dost guide my feet!
blest, To yonder home of sweet e-ter - - nal rest!

130. He Has Come.

"Rejoice greatly, O daughter of Zion; . . . behold, thy King cometh unto thee."—Zech. 9: 9.

Mrs. J. H. Knowles.   Mrs. Joseph F. Knapp.

1. He has come! He has come! my Redeemer has come, He has taken my heart as His own chosen home; At last I have giv-en the welcome He sought, He has come and His coming all gladness has brought.

2. He has come! He has come! my Love and my Lord, Ev-'ry tho't of my being is swayed by His word; He has come! and He rules in the realm of my soul, And His sceptre is love, O blessed control!

3. He has come! He has come! O happiest heart, He has giv-en His word that He will not depart; No trouble can en-ter, no e-vil can come, To the heart where the God of peace has His home.

4. He has come to a-bide, and ho-ly must be The place where my Lord deigns to banquet with me; And this is my prayer, Lord, since Thou art come, Make meet for Thy presence my heart as Thy home.

CHORUS.

Joy! joy is mine, My Saviour divine, Comes to abide with me, with me; *rit.* with me, Comes to abide, ever to abide, My own loving Saviour abideth with me.

By permission.   Copyright.

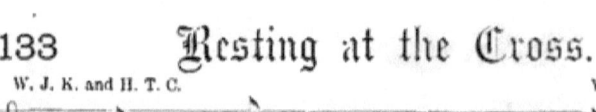

133. Resting at the Cross.

W. J. K. and H. T. C.
Wm. J. Kirkpatrick.

1. To the cross of Christ, my Saviour, I had brought my weary soul,
2. At the cross, while meekly bowing, Je-sus, smiling, bade me live;
3. At the cross, while living dai-ly, Further light shone in my soul,
4. At the cross I'm calm-ly rest-ing, Ev-'ry moment now is sweet;

Burdened, faint, and broken-heart-ed, Praying, "Je-sus, make me whole."
"I have died for your transgressions, And I free-ly all forgive."
And my Saviour gently whispered, Now "thy faith hath made thee whole."
I am tast-ing of His glo-ry, I am resting at His feet.

CHORUS.

Glo-ry, glo-ry be to Je-sus, I am counting all but dross,
I have found a full sal-va-tion, I am resting at the cross;
I'm resting, I'm resting, I'm resting at the cross.
at the cross, at the cross,

By permission. 88 Copyright.

134. Companionship with Jesus.

MARY D. JAMES.   W. J. KIRKPATRICK.

1. Oh, blessed fellow-ship divine! Oh, joy supremely sweet! Com-pan-ionship with Je-sus here Makes life with bliss replete: In un-ion with the pur-est One, I find my heav'n on earth be-gun.
2. I'm walking close to Je-sus' side; So close that I can hear The soft-est whispers of His love In fel-lowship so dear, And feel His great Al-mighty hand Protects me in this hos-tile land.
3. I'm leaning on His loving breast, Along life's happy way; My path, il-lumined by His smiles, Grows brighter day by day: No foes, no woes my heart can fear, With my Almighty Friend so near.
4. I know His sheltering wings of love Are always o'er me spread; And though the storms may fiercely rage, All calm and free from dread, My peaceful spir-it ev-er sings, "I'll trust the covert of Thy wings.

REFRAIN.

Oh, wondrous bliss! oh, joy sublime! I've Jesus with me all the time!
Oh, wondrous bliss! oh, joy sublime! I've Jesus with me all the time!

From "Songs of Joy and Gladness," by permission.   Copyright.

136. I Am Free.

E. A. H. REV. B. C. OYLER.

1. Now the chains of sin are broken, I am free, I'm free;
   Christ the word of power has spoken, Un-to me, to me.
2. Soon as I by faith received Him, Fled the night, the night;
   In the moment I believed Him, Came the light, the light.

CHORUS.
Hal-le-lu-jah! hal-le-lu-jah! Jesus died for me; Hal-le-lu-jah! hal-le-lu-jah! I am free, I'm free.

3 All the fetters that oppressed me
   Now are riven, are riven;
   With His precious love He blessed me,
   This to me is heaven.

4 I will tell the wondrous story
   Of His grace and love;
   He has filled my soul with glory,
   Praise the Lord above!

137. He Leadeth Me.

REV. J. H. GILMORE. Ch'd by H. T. C. KEY OF D. (G. H. 51.)

1 He leadeth me! oh, blessed thought,
  Oh, words with heavenly comfort fraught;
  Whate'er I do, where'er I be,
  Still 'tis God's hand that leadeth me.

REF.—He leadeth me! He leadeth me!
  By His own hand He leadeth me;
  His faithful follower I would be,
  For by His hand He leadeth me.

2 Lord, I would clasp Thy hand in mine,
  Nor ever murmur nor repine—
  Content, whatever lot I see,
  Since 'tis my God that leadeth me.

3 And when my task on earth is done,
  When, by Thy grace, the victory's won,
  With saints above my song shall be,
  Still 'tis my God that leadeth me.

138. I Have a Saviour.

S. O. CLUFF. KEY OF G. (G. H. 11.)

1 I have a Saviour, He's pleading in glory,
  A dear, loving Saviour, though earth friends be few;
  And now He is watching in tenderness o'er me,
  And oh that my Saviour were your Saviour too.

CHORUS.
For you I am praying, For you I am praying,
For you I am praying, I'm praying for you.

2 I have a peace: it is calm as a river—
  A peace that the friends of the world never knew,
  My Saviour alone is its Author and Giver,
  And oh, could I know it was given to you!

3 I have a Father: to me He has given
  A hope for eternity, blessed and true;
  And soon will He call me to meet Him in heaven,
  But oh that He'd let me bring you with me too.

4 When Jesus has found you, tell others the story,
  That my loving Saviour is your Saviour too;
  Then pray that your Saviour may bring them to glory,
  And prayer will be answered—'twas answered for you!

140. Since I've Trusted Him.

F. A. B.
F. A. BLACKMER.

1. Once I tho't I walked with Jesus, Yet such changeful feelings had;
2. But He called me closer to Him, Bade my doubting, fearing, cease;
3. Now, I'm trusting every moment, Nothing less can be e-nough;

Sometimes trusting, sometimes doubting, Sometimes joyful, sometimes sad.
And when I had ful-ly yielded, Filled my soul with perfect peace.
And the Saviour bears me gently O'er those places once so rough.

CHORUS.

Oh, the peace the Saviour gives, Peace I nev-er knew be-fore;
And my way has brighter grown, Since I've learned to trust Him more.

By permission.

141. Blest be the Tie That Binds.

J. FAWCETT.
TUNE: G. H. 114. KEY OF F.

1 Blest be the tie that binds
  Our hearts in Christian love:
  The fellowship of kindred minds
  Is like to that above.

2 Before our Father's throne—
  We pour our ardent prayers;
  Our fears, our hopes, our aims are
  Our comforts and our cares. [one—

3 From sorrow, toil, and pain,
  And sin we shall be free;
  And perfect love and friendship
  Through all eternity. [reign

142. Nearer the Cross.

Mrs. Valenstyne. Arranged. Mrs. J. F. Knapp, by per.

1. Nearer the cross, my heart can say, I'm coming nearer;
Nearer the cross, from day to day, I'm coming nearer.
Nearer the cross where Jesus died,
Nearer the fountain's crimson tide,
Nearer my Saviour's wounded side, I'm coming nearer, I'm coming nearer.

2 Nearer the Christian's mercy-seat,
Feasting my soul on manna sweet,
Stronger in faith, more clear I see
Jesus, who gave Himself for me,
Nearer to Him I still would be,
Still coming nearer.

3 Nearer in prayer my hope aspires
Deeper the love my soul desires,
Nearer the end of toil and care,
Nearer the joy my soul shall share,
Nearer the crown I soon shall wear,
I'm coming nearer.

143. Glory to His Name.

"I will glorify Thy Name forevermore."

Rev. E. A. Hoffman. Arranged. Rev. J. H. Stockton.

1. Down at the cross where my Saviour died, Down where for cleansing from
2. I am so wondrously saved from sin, Jesus so sweetly a-
3. Oh, precious fountain, that saves from sin, I am so glad I have
4. Come to this fountain so rich and sweet; Cast thy poor soul at the

Glory to His Name—Concluded.

sin I cried; There to my heart was the blood applied; Glory to His
bides within; There at the cross where He took me in; Glory to His
en-tered in; There Jesus saves me and keeps me clean, Glory to His
Saviour's feet; Trust Him to-day, and be made complete; Glory to His

D.S.—There to my heart was the blood applied; Glo-ry to His

Fine. CHORUS.

name. Glo-ry to His name, Glo-ry to His name;

name.

By permission.

144 Christ, the Solid Rock.

Rev. E. Mote. Arranged

1. { My hope is built on nothing less Than Jesus' blood and righteousness; }
   { I dare not trust the sweetest frame, But wholly lean on Jesus' name. }
2. { When darkness seems to veil His face, I rest on His unchanging grace; }
   { In ev-'ry high and stormy gale, My an-chor holds within the vail. }

D.S.—On Christ, the sol-id Rock, I stand, All oth-er ground is sinking sand.

CHORUS.

On Christ, the sol-id Rock, I stand, All other ground is sinking sand.

3 His oath, His covenant, His blood,
 Support me in the 'whelming flood;
 When all around my soul gives
  way,
 He then is all my hope and 'stay.

4 When He shall come with trumpet
  sound,
 O, I shall then in Him be found;
 Saved by His grace and that alone,
 Faultless to stand before His throne.

145. Cleansing Wave.

PHŒBE PALMER. MRS. J. F. KNAPP, by permission.

1 Oh, now I see the cleansing wave!
  The fountain deep and wide;
  Jesus, my Lord, mighty to save,
  Points to His wounded side.

CHORUS.
  The cleansing stream, I see, I see!
  I trust, and oh, it cleanseth me!
  Oh, praise the Lord! it cleanseth me;
  It cleanseth me—yes, cleanseth me.

2 I see the new creation rise;
  I hear the speaking blood!

3 It speaks! polluted nature dies!
  Sinks 'neath the cleansing flood.

3 I rise to walk in heaven's own light,
  Above the world of sin,
  With heart made pure and garments white,
  And Christ enthroned within.

4 Amazing grace! 'tis heaven below,
  To feel the blood applied;
  And Jesus, only Jesus, know,
  My Jesus crucified.

146   I Know That My Redeemer Lives.

C. WESLEY.   TUNE: No. 145.

1 I know that my Redeemer lives
  And ever prays for me;
  A token of His love He gives—
  A pledge of liberty.

CHORUS.
  The cleansing stream, I see, I see!
  I trust, and oh, it cleanseth me!
  Oh, praise the Lord, it cleanseth me;
  It cleanseth me—yes, cleanseth me.

2 I find Him lifting up my head;
  He brings salvation near;

  His presence makes me free indeed,
  And He will soon appear.

3 When God is mine, and I am His,
  Of paradise possessed,
  I taste unutterable bliss
  And everlasting rest.

4 Thou only know'st, who didst obtain,
  And die to make it known,
  The great salvation now explain,
  And perfect us in one.

147   Draw Me Nearer.

F. J. CROSBY.   TUNE: G. H. 138. KEY OF A FLAT.

1 I am Thine, O Lord, I have heard Thy voice,
  And it told Thy love to me;
  But I long to rise in the arms of faith,
  And be closer drawn to Thee.

CHORUS.
  Draw me nearer, (nearer,) nearer, blessed Lord,
  To the cross where Thou hast died;
  Draw me nearer, nearer, nearer, blessed Lord,
  To Thy precious, bleeding side.

2 Sanctify me now to Thy service, Lord,
  By the power of grace divine;

  Let my soul look up with a steadfast hope,
  And my will be lost in Thine.

3 O the pure delight of a single hour
  That before Thy throne I spend;
  When I kneel in prayer, and with Thee, my God,
  I commune as friend with friend.

4 There are depths of love that I cannot know
  Till I cross the narrow sea;
  There are heights of joy that I cannot reach
  Till I rest in peace with Thee.

148 Beulah Land.
EDGAR PAGE. (G. H. 305.)

1 I've reached the land of corn and wine,
  And all its riches freely mine;
  Here shines undimm'd one blissful day,
  For all my night has passed away.

CHORUS.
  O Beulah land, sweet Beulah land,
  As on thy highest mount I stand,
  I look away across the sea, [me,
  Where mansions are prepared for
  And view the shining glory shore,
  My heaven, my home, for evermore!

2 The Saviour comes and walks with me,
  And sweet communion here have we;
  He gently leads me with His hand,
  For this is heaven's border land.

3 The zephyrs seem to float to me
  Sweet sounds of heaven's melody,
  As angels, with the white-robed throng,
  Join in the sweet redemption song.

149 Happy Day.
DODDRIDGE. (G. H. 305.)

1 O happy day, that fixed my choice
    On Thee, my Saviour and my God!
  Well may this glowing heart rejoice,
    And tell its rapture all abroad.

CHORUS.
  O happy day, O happy day,
  When Jesus washed my sins way;
  He taught me how to watch and pray,
  And live rejoicing every day;
  O happy day, O happy day,
  When Jesus washed my sins away.

2 O happy bond that seals my vows
    To Him who merits all my love;
  Let cheerful anthems fill His house,
    While to that sacred shrine I move.

3 'Tis done, the great transaction's done—
    I am my Lord's and He is mine;
  He drew me, and I followed on,
    Charmed to confess the voice divine.

4 Now rest, my long-divided heart;
    Fixed on this blissful centre, rest;
  Nor ever from thy Lord depart,
    With Him of every good possessed.

5 High heaven that heard the solemn vow,
    That vow, renewed, shall daily hear,
  Till in life's latest hour I bow,
    And bless in death a bond so dear.

150 Why I Love Jesus.
(S. O. G. N. 9.)

1 Would you know why I love Jesus?
    Why He is so dear to me?
  'Tis because my blessed Jesus
    From my sins has ransomed me.

CHORUS.
  This is why I love my Jesus,
    This is why I love Him so;
  He atoned for my transgression,
    He has washed me white as show.

2 Would you know why I love Jesus?
    Why He is so dear to me?
  'Tis because the blood of Jesus
    Fully saves and cleanses me.

3 Would you know why I love Jesus?
    Why He is so dear to me?
  'Tis because, amid temptation,
    He supports and strengthens me.

4 Would you know why I love Jesus?
    Why He is so dear to me?
  'Tis because, my Friend and Saviour,
    He will ever, ever be.

151 He Took Me In.
(G. H. 305.)

1 Although I wandered far from God,
    And trampled on my Saviour's blood,
  When I returned, confessed my sin,
    My dear Redeemer took me in.

CHORUS.
  He took me in, He took me in,
    And freely pardoned all my sin.
  Though far away from Him I strayed,
    And His salvation long delayed;
  Yet, oh! when I confessed my sin,
    My dear Redeemer took me in.

2 I never shall forget the day
    When Jesus met me in the way;
  With pity beaming in His eye,
    He looked at me so tenderly.

3 My many sins were all forgiven,
    And I was made an heir of heaven
  The peace of God then filled my soul,
    And I was made completely whole.

4 All glory to the bleeding Lamb,
    Whose dying love my heart o'ercame
  My life, my all I owe to Him,
    Who did my precious soul redeem.

153. It is Good to be Here.

C. WESLEY. — Adapted by H. T. C.

1. O how happy are they, Who the Saviour obey, And have
  Tongue can never express The sweet comfort and peace Of a
  laid up their treasures above. . . . .
  . . . . soul in its earliest love.

D.C.—And the light streaming down makes the pathway all clear, It is
  good for us, Lord, to be here.

CHORUS.
It is good to be here, It is good to be here, Thy perfect love drives away fear,

2 This sweet comfort was mine,
  When the favor Divine [Lamb;
  I received through the blood of the
  When my heart first believed,
  What a joy I received—
  What a heaven in Jesus' Name!

3 Jesus, all the day long,
  Was my joy and my song:
  O that all His salvation might see;
  "He hath loved me," I cried,
  "He hath suffered and died,
  To redeem even rebels like me."

4 O the rapturous height
  Of that holy delight
  Which I felt in the life-giving blood;
  Of my Saviour possessed,
  I was perfectly blest,
  As if filled with the fulness of God.

154. O How Happy are We.

C. WESLEY. — TUNE: No. 153.

1 O how happy are we,
  Who in Jesus agree,
  To expect His return from above!
  We sit under our Vine,
  And delightfully join
  In the praise of His excellent love.
  CHO.—It is good to be here, etc.

2 O how pleasant and sweet
  Is His name when we meet,
  Is His fruit to our spiritual taste!
  We are banqueting here
  On angelical cheer,
  And the joys that eternally last.

3 All invited by Him,
  We now drink of the stream,
  Ever flowing in bliss from the throne.
  Who in Jesus believe,
  We the Spirit receive,
  That proceeds from the Father and Son.

4 We remember the word
  Of our crucified Lord,
  When He went to prepare us a place:
  "I will come in that day
  And transport you away,
  And admit to the sight of My face"

155. Happy in the Lord.

1. { A pilgrim and a stranger here, happy, happy, happy, I seek the home to
   { Dear friends have reached that blissful shore, happy, happy, happy, They sorrow not and
   pilgrims dear, hap-py in the Lord,
   sigh no more, hap-py in the Lord. } We'll cross the riv-er of Jor-dan,
   happy, happy, happy, happy, Cross the river of Jor-dan, happy in the Lord.

2 I leave this world of sin behind, happy, etc.,
  That better home in heaven to find, happy, etc.,
  Fair lands are here, and houses fair, happy, etc.,
  But fairer is my home up there, happy, etc.

3 O happy day when first Thy love, happy, etc.,
  Began our grateful hearts to move, happy, etc.;
  And gazing on Thy wondrous cross, happy, etc.,
  We saw all else as worthless dross, happy, etc.

4 O happy day! when we shall see, happy, etc.,
  And fix our longing eyes on Thee, happy, etc.,
  On Thee, our Light, our Life, our Love, happy, etc.,
  Our All below, our Heaven above, happy, etc.

156. Full Salvation.

Miss Boole. Arranged.

L. M. R. Changed.

1 Precious Jesus, Thou hast saved me:
  Thine, and only Thine, I am:
  Oh! the cleansing blood has reached me,
  Glory, glory to the Lamb.

  CHORUS.
  Glory, glory, Jesus saves me,
  Glory, glory to the Lamb!
  Oh! the cleansing blood has reached me,
  Glory, glory to the Lamb.

2 Long my yearning heart was trying
  To enjoy this perfect rest,
  But I gave all trying over:
  Simply trusting, I was blest.

3 Consecrated to Thy service,
  I will live and die for Thee;
  I will witness to Thy glory
  Of salvation full and free.

4 Glory to the Lord that bought me!
  Glory to His saving power!
  Glory to the Lord that keeps me!
  Glory, glory evermore!

We Shall Reap By and By—Concluded.

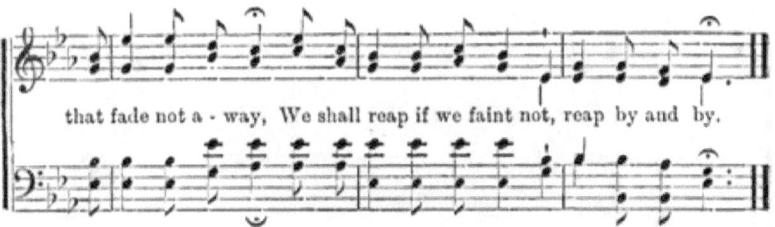

that fade not a-way, We shall reap if we faint not, reap by and by.

163 Sowing in the Morning.

K. Shaw. Arranged.   Tune: G. H. 370.

1 Sowing in the morning, sowing seeds of kindness,
   Sowing in the noontide and the dewy eve;
   Waiting for the harvest, and the time of reaping,
     We shall come rejoicing, bringing in the sheaves.

        Chorus.
     ‖: Bringing in the sheaves, :‖
      We shall come rejoicing,
      Bringing in the sheaves.

2 Sowing in the sunshine, sowing in the shadows,
   Fearing neither clouds nor winter's chilling breeze;
   By and by the harvest, and the labor ended,
     We shall come rejoicing, bringing in the sheaves.

3 Going forth with weeping, sowing for the Master,
   Tho' the loss sustained our spirit often grieves;
   When our labor's over, He will bid us welcome,
     We shall come rejoicing, bringing in the sheaves.

164 Work To-Day.

A. L. Walter.   Tune: D. H. 89.

1 Work, for the night is coming;
   Work through the morning hours;
   Work while the dew is sparkling;
   Work 'mid springing flowers;
   Work when the day grows brighter;
   Work in the glowing sun;
   Work, for the night is coming,
   When man's work is done.

2 Work, for the night is coming;
   Work through the sunny noon;
   Fill brightest hours with labor;
   Rest comes sure and soon.

   Give every flying minute
   Something to keep in store;
   Work, for the night is coming,
   When man works no more.

3 Work, for the night is coming,
   Under the sunset skies;
   While their bright tints are glowing,
   Work for daylight flies;
   Work till the last beam fadeth,—
   Fadeth to shine no more;
   Work, while the night is dark'ning,
   When man's work is o'er.

165 Rescue the Perishing.

F. J. Crosby.   Tune: G. H. 18.

1 Rescue the perishing,
   Care for the dying,
   Snatch them in pity from sin and the grave;
   Weep o'er the erring ones;
   Lift up the fallen,
   Tell them of Jesus, the mighty to save.

        Chorus.
     Rescue the perishing,
     Care for the dying;
     Jesus is merciful,
     Jesus will save.

2 Though they are slighting Him,
   Still He is waiting,
   Waiting the penitent child to receive.
   Plead with them earnestly,
   Plead with them gently;
   He will forgive if they only believe.

3 Down in the human heart,
   Crushed by the tempter,
   Feelings lie buried that grace can restore;
   Touched by a loving heart,
   Wakened by kindness,
   Chords that were broken will vibrate once more.

4 Rescue the perishing,
   Duty demands it;
   Strength for thy labor the Lord will provide;
   Back to the narrow way
   Patiently win them,
   Tell the poor wanderer a Saviour has died.

166. The Field of Christian Duty.

FANNY J. CROSBY. Arranged. JNO. R. SWENEY.

1. In the field of Christian duty there's a place for every one, And the
2. O, that field of Christian duty all a-round us we may find, And we
3. Yes, there's work to do for Jesus,—there are sinners to reclaim,—We must
4. In that field of Christian duty we are toiling not in vain, For the

moments like the shadows glide away; But there's work to do for Jesus, and a
need not turn our footsteps far away; There are weary ones to comfort, there are
scatter love and kindness in their way; With a patient, humble spirit we must
Saviour will reward us by and by; Oh, 'tis worth our strongest efforts, more than

work that must be done, From the dawning till the closing of the day.
bro-ken hearts to bind, From the dawning till the closing of the day.
la-bor in His name, From the dawning till the closing of the day.
worth a life of praise, When we think of yonder mansion in the sky.

CHORUS.

Sowing, praying, trusting, waiting, Till the coming of the
Sowing, praying, trusting, waiting,

Master we shall see; Then among the tried and faithful in the
we shall see,

By permission. Copyright.

The Field of Christian Duty—*Concluded.*

garner of the Lord, What a gathering of the faithful there will be.

167 Fall Into Line.

Rev. E. A. Hoffman. Arranged.   J. H. Tenney.

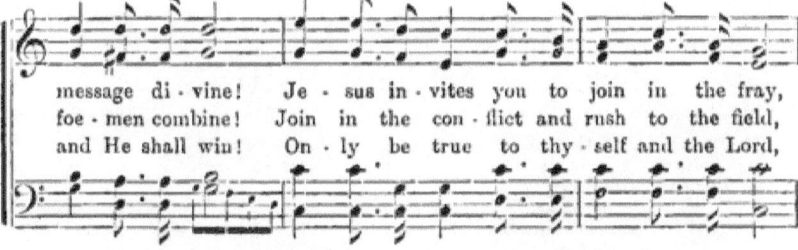

1. Fall in-to line, Christians, fall in-to line! Hearken to me, to the
2. Fall in-to line, Christians, fall in-to line! See how the hosts of the
3. Fall in-to line, Christians, fall in-to line! God is om-ni-po-tent

message di-vine! Je-sus in-vites you to join in the fray,
foe-men combine! Join in the con-flict and rush to the field,
and He shall win! On-ly be true to thy-self and the Lord,

CHORUS.

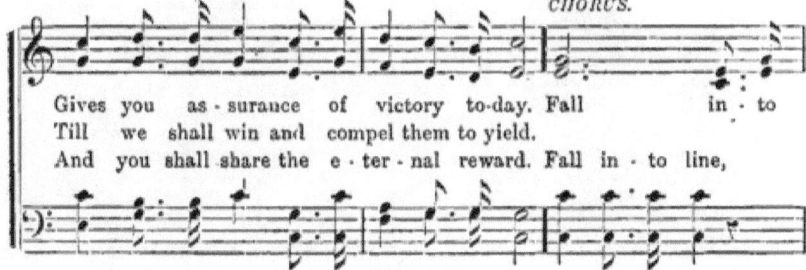

Gives you as-surance of victory to-day. Fall   in-to
Till we shall win and compel them to yield.
And you shall share the e-ter-nal reward. Fall in-to line,

Fall Into Line—Concluded.

line, Christians fall in - to line,
fall in - to line. Fall in - to line, Christians, fall in - to line!

On to the bat - tle, for Je - sus shall win!
On to the battle, Fall into line! Jesus shall win! Fierce is the war-

fare with Satan to-day; Arm for the conflict and march to the fray.

168 Christian Soldier's Battle-Song.

S. B. GOULD.   TUNE: No. 169.

1 Onward, Christian soldiers,
  Marching as to war,
Looking unto Jesus,
  Who is gone before.
Christ, the Royal Master,
  Leads against the foe;
Forward into battle,
  See His banners go!

CHORUS.
Onward, Christian soldiers,
  Marching as to war,
Looking unto Jesus,
  Who is gone before.

2 Like a mighty army
  Moves the Church of God;
Christians, we are treading
  Where the saints have trod;
We are not divided,
  All one body we,

One in hope and doctrine,
  One in charity

3 Crowns and thrones may perish,
  Kingdoms rise and wane,
But the Church of Jesus
  Constant will remain;
Gates of hell can never
  'Gainst that Church prevail,
We have Christ's own promise,
  Which can never fail.

4 Onward, then, ye people,
  Join our happy throng;
Blend with ours your voices
  In the triumph song.
Glory, praise, and honor,
  Men and angels sing,
Through the countless ages,
  Unto Christ our King.

172. The Pearly Gate.

Duet.
"Strive to enter in at the strait gate."

ELLEN OLIVER. E. B. SMITH.

1. The door of God's mercy is o-pen To all who are weary of sin,
2. The world is e'er wantonly wooing Your soul from the ways of the blest,
3. So many who hear the glad message, Will never its mandates obey,
4. Sad hearts there will surely be moaning Outside of the gateway of life,
5. The door of God's mercy is o-pen, In-viting-ly o-pen to all,

And Jesus is patiently waiting, Still waiting, to welcome you in.
But Jesus is tender-ly bidding You turn to His heavenly rest.
But turn from the precious, dear pleadings, And wilfully wander away.
And praying to Him they rejected When earth with gay pleasure was rife.
Who list to the voice of the Master, And hearing shall heed His sweet call.

CHORUS.

Come, says the Saviour, Come enter the gate, I watch by the portals both ear-ly and late, Lest some precious soul, Not far from the goal, Should wander away into darkness and hate, And miss it forever, the pearly gate.

175. When the Harvest is Past.

S. F. Smith.   H. H. McGranahan.

1. When the harvest is past and the summer is gone, And summons and prayers shall be o'er, When the beams cease to break of the blest Sabbath morn, And Jesus invites thee no more.
2. When the rich gales of mercy no longer shall blow, The gospel no message declare; Sinner, how can'st thou bear the deep wailings of woe? How suffer the night of despair?
3. When the holy have gone to the regions of peace, To dwell in the mansions above, Where their harmony makes, in the fulness of bliss, Their song to the Saviour they love.
4. Say, O sinner, that livest at rest and secure, Who fearest no trouble to come, Can thy spirit the swellings of sorrow endure, Or bear the impenitent's doom?

CHORUS.

When the harvest is past and the summer is gone, When the harvest is past and the summer is gone, and Jesus invites thee no more.

By permission.

177. Eternity!—Where?

A young man was working alone in a large room in which was a big clock, the loud ticking of which seemed to frame itself into the words, "Eternity!—where?" Unable to endure any longer the reflections thus awakened, he arose and stopped the clock; but the question, "Eternity!—where?" still so haunted him, that he threw down his work, and hurrying home, determined that he would not allow anything to engage his thoughts till he could satisfactorily answer that searching question, "Eternity!—where?"

Jno. R. Sweney.

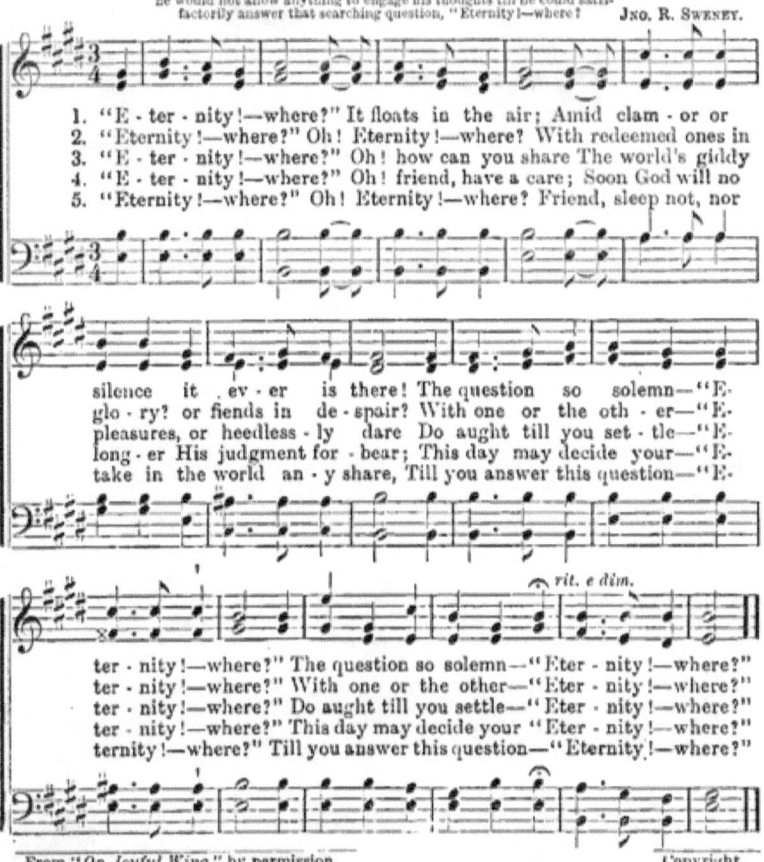

1. "E-ter-nity!—where?" It floats in the air; Amid clam-or or silence it ever is there! The question so solemn—"Eter-nity!—where?" The question so solemn—"Eter-nity!—where?"
2. "Eternity!—where?" Oh! Eternity!—where? With redeemed ones in glo-ry? or fiends in de-spair? With one or the oth-er—"E-ter-nity!—where?" With one or the other—"Eter-nity!—where?"
3. "E-ter-nity!—where?" Oh! how can you share The world's giddy pleasures, or heedless-ly dare Do aught till you set-tle—"E-ter-nity!—where?" Do aught till you settle—"Eter-nity!—where?"
4. "E-ter-nity!—where?" Oh! friend, have a care; Soon God will no long-er His judgment for-bear; This day may decide your—"E-ter-nity!—where?" This day may decide your "Eter-nity!—where?"
5. "Eternity!—where?" Oh! Eternity!—where? Friend, sleep not, nor take in the world an-y share, Till you answer this question—"E-ter-nity!—where?" Till you answer this question—"Eternity!—where?"

From "*On Joyful Wing*," by permission.   Copyright.

178. Almost Persuaded.

P. P. Bliss.   Tune: G. H. 75.   Key of G.

1 "Almost persuaded" now to believe;
    "Almost persuaded" Christ to receive;
  Seems now some soul to say,
    "Go, Spirit, go Thy way,
  Some more convenient day
    On Thee I'll call."

2 "Almost persuaded," come, come to-day;
    "Almost persuaded," turn not away.
  Jesus invites you here,
  Angels are lingering near,
  Prayers rise from hearts so dear;
    "O wanderer, come."

3 "Almost persuaded," harvest is past!
    "Almost persuaded," doom comes at last!
  "Almost" cannot avail;
  "Almost" is but to fail!
  Sad, sad, that bitter wail—
    "Almost—*but lost!*"

179 Gathering Home.

"Ye shall be gathered one by one, O ye children of Israel."—Ps. 27: 12.

MARY LESLIE. Changed by CROSSLEY BROS. W. A. OGDEN.

1. They're gathering homeward from every land, One by one, one by one;
2. Be - fore they rest they pass thro' the strife, One by one, one by one;
3. We, too, shall come to the ri - ver side, One by one, one by one;
4. Je - sus, Re - deemer, we look to Thee, One by one, one by one;

As their weary feet touch the shining strand, Yes, one by one.
Through the Jordan of death they en - ter life, Yes, one by one.
We are near - er its wa - ters each e - ventide, Yes, one by one.
We lift up our voi - ces trust - ing - ly, Yes, one by one.

They rest with their Saviour, receive their crown, Their travel-stained
The wa - ters divide as their feet touch the shore, And exulting in
We have heard and read of the "rushing stream," Oft now and a -
Oh, keep us by grace in the narrow way, Till we have fin-

garments are all laid down; They receive the fair mansion the
Je - sus their spirits pass o'er; The waves to some may run
gain thro' our life's deep dream, But we'll fear not to enter with
ish - ed our life's short day, Then when one by one to the

By permission. Copyright.

Gathering Home—Concluded.

Lord did prepare For all who the glory with Him shall share.
fiercely and wild, But they are not so to the un-defiled.
Christ as our guide, For He will sure-ly the stream di-vide.
ri-ver we've come, We know Thou wilt gath-er us safely home.

REFRAIN.
Gathering home! gathering home! Crossing the ri-ver one by one!
Gathering home! gathering home, yes, one by one!

NOTE.—The passage of the Jordan to the promised land by the Israelites, as a type of the Christian's death, is greatly misrepresented both in poetry and prose. We hear much of "fording the river," "death's cold stream," "dismal flood," "swelling current," "dark river," etc. Such expressions are entirely contrary to both scripture and experience, and give wrong ideas of death which frighten many Christians from the shore. The waters divided *when reached*, and the people, without fear, passed triumphantly "over on dry ground." (See Joshua iii. 14-17; iv. 1-18.) Christians *when they come to death* are able to say with good Bishop Haven: "There is no river here." My brother (D. O. C.) and I have arranged the above hymn to accord with scripture and experience. Let each one who reads this be a Christian, march on happily in the path of duty and, as with others,

When you reach the verge of Jordan
He'll its waters *then* divide,
Bear you through in faith triumphant,
Land you safe on Canaan's side.—H. T. C

180 The Crowning Day.

TUNE: G. H. 416. KEY of A FLAT.

1 Our Lord is now rejected
  And by the world disowned,
By the many still neglected,
  And by the few enthroned,
But soon He'll come in glory,
  The hour is drawing nigh, [and by.
For the crowning day is coming by

CHORUS.
Oh, the crowning day is coming,
  Is coming by and by,
When our Lord shall come in "power,"
  And "glory" from on high;
Oh, the glorious sight will gladden
  Each waiting, watchful eye, [and by.
In the crowning day that's coming by

2 The heavens shall glow with splendor,
  But brighter far than they
The saints shall shine in glory,
  As Christ shall them array.
The beauty of the Saviour
  Shall dazzle every eye, [and by.
In the crowning day that's coming by

3 Let all that look for hasten
  The coming joyful day,
By earnest consecration,
  To walk the narrow way,
By gathering in the lost ones,
  For whom our Lord did die,
For the crowning day that's coming by
  and by.

182. The Judgment Day.

Arranged by H. T. C.

1. { The judgment day is coming,
     The judgment day is coming, } com-ing, com-ing, Oh, ... that great day.

CHORUS.

Let us haste a-way to Je-sus, And find in Him sal-va-tion,
Let us haste a-way to Je-sus, And sound the ju-bi-lee.

2 We'll hear the trumpet sounding, etc.
3 We'll see the Judge descending, etc.
4 We'll see the dead arising etc.
5 We'll see the world assembled, etc.
6 We'll hear the sentence uttered, etc.
7 Then repentance will be useless, etc.
8 For no pardon will be granted, etc.

9 We'll hear the wicked wailing,
  For they hasted not to Jesus, nor, etc.
10 We'll hear the righteous shouting,
   For they fled away to Jesus, and, etc.
11 You'd better come to Jesus
   Just now while you may.

183. Rest for the Weary.

Arr. by R. M. McIntosh. By permission.

1. In the Christian's home in glo-ry, There re-mains a land of rest;
2. He is fit-ting up my mansion, Which e-ter-nal-ly shall stand,
3. Pain and sick-ness ne'er shall en-ter, Grief nor woe my lot shall share,
4. Sing, O, sing, ye heirs of glo-ry—Shout your tri-umphs as you go;

There my Saviour's gone before me, To ful fil my soul's re-quest.
For my stay shall not be transient In that ho-ly hap-py land.
But, in that ce-les-tial cen-tre, I a crown of life shall wear.
Zi-on's gates will o-pen for you, Ye shall find an en-trance through.

CHORUS.

{ There is rest for the wea-ry—There is rest for the wea-ry—
  On the other side of Jor-dan, In the sweet fields of E-den, }

There is rest for the wea-ry—There is rest for you.
Where the tree of life is blooming—There is rest for you.

184. To That City Will You Go?

Mrs. M. D. C. Slade.   Dr. A. B. Everett.

1. Where the jasper walls are beaming, Where the pearly portals are glowing;
2. O - pen are the shining por - tals, Shut by night or day are they never,
3. In that many-mansioned dwelling, Je - sus one for you is pre - paring;
4. There shall be no day's declin - ing, Tho' no sun nor moon light the heaven;

Where the golden street is gleaming, Where the crystal waters are flowing:—
With the glo - ri - fied immor - tals, Will you dwell within them forever?
Where hosannas glad are swelling, Will you come their joy sweetly sharing?
From amidst the throne is shin - ing Glory from the Lord freely given.

CHORUS.

Down beside that wondrous ri - ver, Where the trees of healing grow

We shall meet and live for - ev - er, To that Cit - y will you go?

From "Prayer and Praise," by permission.

Shall I Meet You?—*Concluded.*

meet you In the hap-py land beyond the sky?
meet you by - and - by?

---

187. I Shall be Satisfied.

Dr. H. Bonar.
Moderato.
Rev. T. C. Neal.

1. When I shall wake in that fair morn of morns, Af-ter whose dawning never night returns, And with whose glory day eternal burns, I shall be satisfied.
2. When I shall see Thy glo-ry face to face, When in Thine arms Thou wilt Thy child embrace, When Thou shalt open all Thy stores of grace, I shall be [satisfied.
3. When I shall meet with those that I have loved, Clasp in my ea-ger arms the long removed, And find how faithful Thou to me hast proved, I shall be [satisfied.
4. When I shall gáze up-on the face of Him Who for me died, with eye no longer dim, And praise Him with the everlasting hymn, I shall be satisfied.

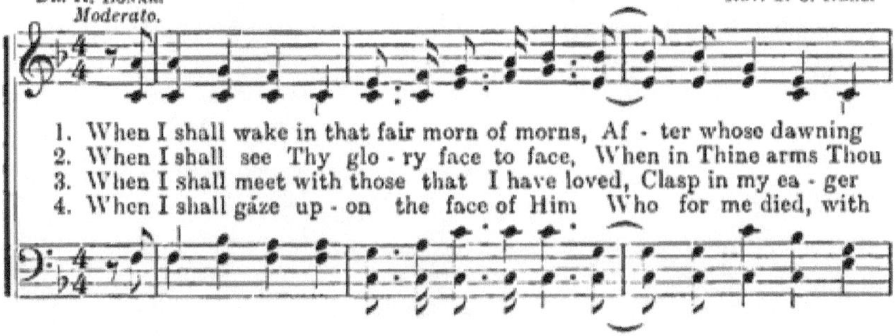

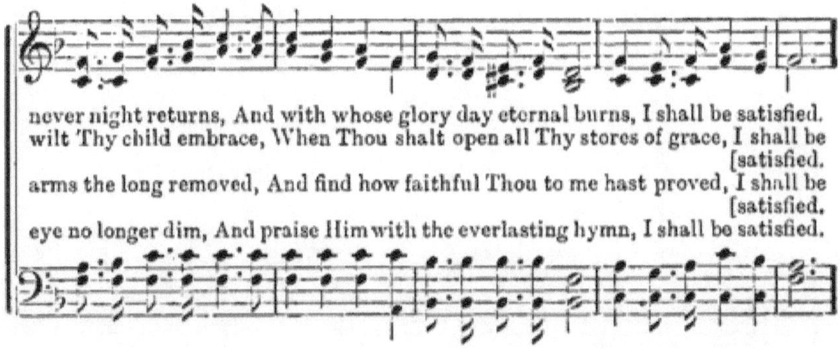

CHORUS.   *rit.*

I shall be satisfied, I shall be satisfied, I shall be satisfied, By-and-by.

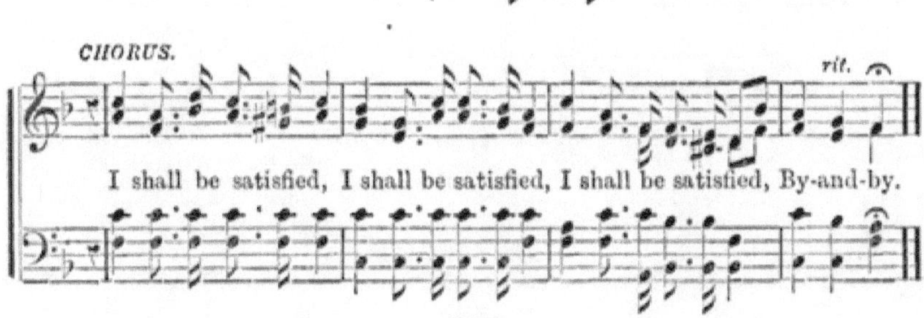

3 We shall gather home at last,
 ‖: Sorrow past, :‖
We shall hold our jewels fast
 In the kingdom.
We shall dwell in perfect light,
 ‖: Holy light, :‖
Never dimmed by tears at night
 In the kingdom.

4 We shall know each other there,
 ‖: Over there, :‖
When our glorious robes we wear,
 In the kingdom.
All that's purest, holiest here,
 ‖: Grows more dear :‖
In the mansions drawing near,
 In the kingdom.

190. One by One.

Rev. E. H. Stokes, D.D.   Jno. R. Sweney.

1. One by one, our loved ones slowly Pass beyond the bounds of time;
2. One by one, soon we shall gather, Not as we have gathered here—
3. One by one, our ranks are thinning—Thinning here but swelling there;
4. Good-bye! hail! the fondly cherished, Tears and joys are ours to day;

One by one, among the ho-ly, Sing the vic-tor's song sublime.
Bowed and broken,—but the rather, In e-ter-nal youth ap-pear.
One by one bright crowns are winning, Crowns they shall forever wear.
Some have gone, and lo! the others Hasten on the shortening way.

CHORUS.

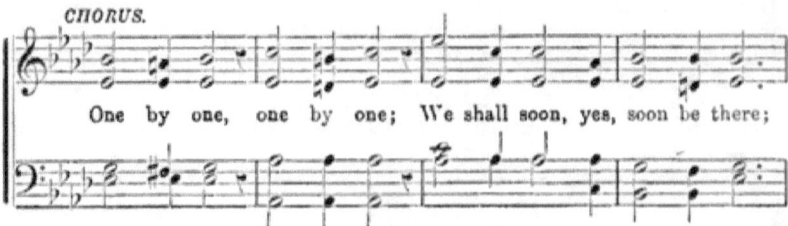

One by one, one by one; We shall soon, yes, soon be there;
One by one, yes, one by one, We shall end-less glo-ry share.

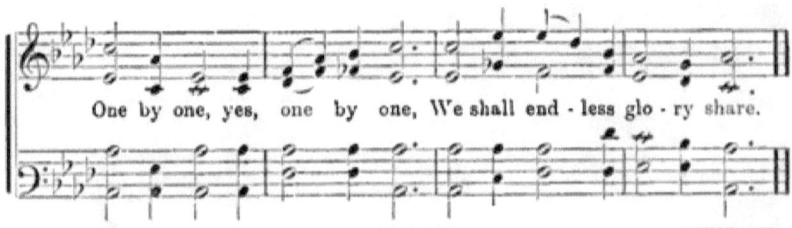

From "Songs of Redeeming Love," by permission.   Copyright.

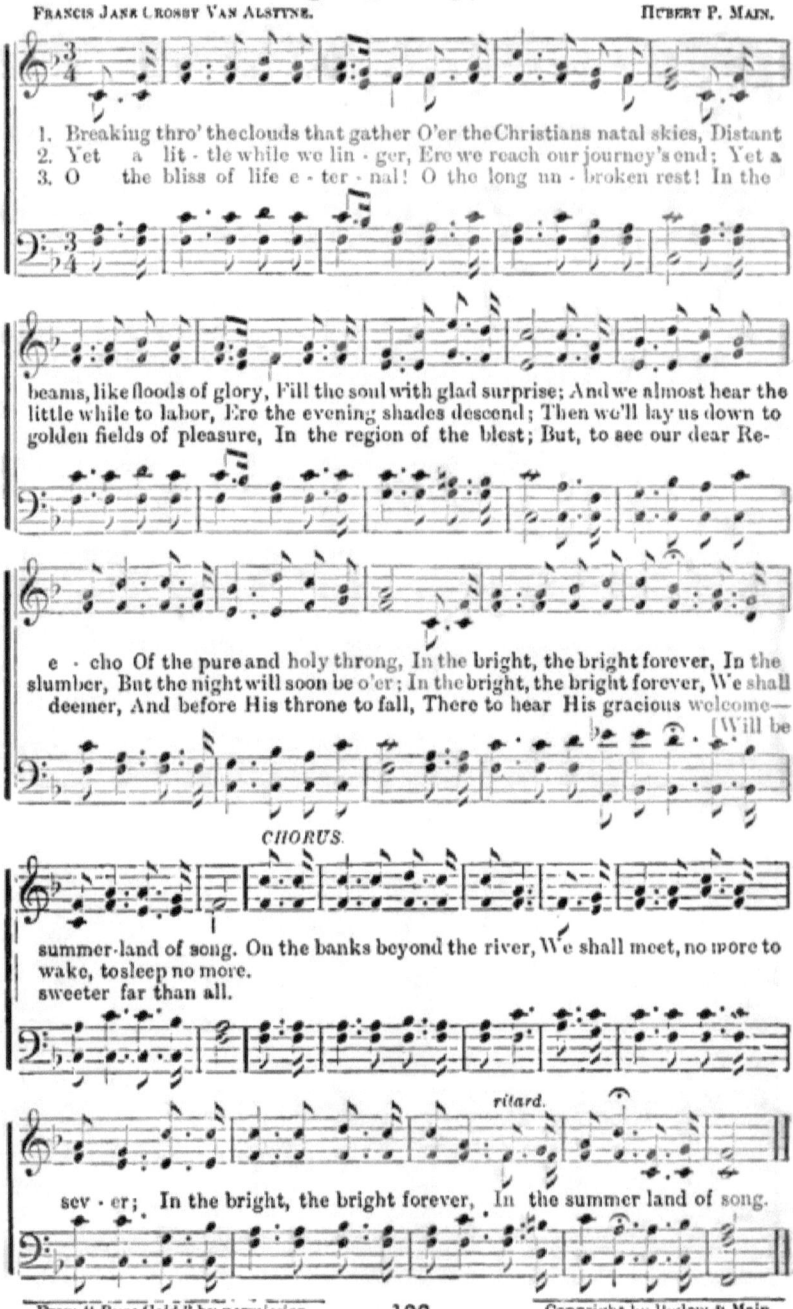

193. No Night in Heaven.

WM. J. KIRKPATRICK.

1. No night shall be in heaven; no gathering gloom Shall o'er that glorious land-
[scape
2. No night shall be in heaven; forbid to sleep, These eyes no more their mournful
3. No night shall be in heaven, but endless noon; No fast-declining sun, no
4. No night shall be in heaven; no darkened room, No bed of death, nor silence

ev - er come; No tears shall fall in sadness o'er those flowers That
vi - gils keep; Their fountains dried, their tears all wiped away, They
waning moon; But there the Lamb shall yield per - petual light, 'Mid
of the tomb, But breez - es ev - er fresh with love and truth Shall

CHORUS.

breathe their fragrance thro' celestial bowers. No night in heaven,
gaze un - dazzled on e - ter - nal day.
pas - tures green and waters ev - er bright.
brace the frame with an im - mor - tal youth. No night in heaven,

No night in heaven, But all is joy and light,—No night in heaven.
No night in heaven,

From "*Songs of Redeeming Love*," by permission. Copyright.

195. Welcome to Glory.

Mrs. P. Palmer. Mrs. J. F. Knapp.

1. O, when shall I sweep thro' the gate, The scenes of mortality o'er,
   What then for my spirit awaits? Will they sing on the glorified shore?
2. When from Calvary's mount I arise, And pass thro' the portals above,
   Will shouts, Welcome home to the skies! Resound thro' the regions of love?
3. Yes! loved ones who knew me below, Who learned the new song with me here,
   In chorus will hail me, I know, And welcome me home, with good cheer.
4. The beautiful gates will unfold, The home of the blood-washed I'll see;
   The city of saints I'll behold! For, O, there's a welcome for me!
5. A sinner made whiter than snow, I'll join in the mighty acclaim,
   And shout thro' the gates as I go, Salvation to God and the Lamb!

CHORUS.

Welcome home! welcome home! A welcome in glory for me;
Welcome home! Welcome home! Welcome home! welcome home! A welcome for me.
Welcome home! Welcome home! Welcome home!

By permission.   Copyright.

196. The Numberless Host.

F. A. Blackmer. F. A. B. Arr. by H. T. C. & W. J. B.

1. When we enter the portals of glory, And the great host of ransomed we see,
2. When we see all the saved of the ages, Who from cruel death partings are free,
3. When we stand by the beautiful river, 'Neath the shade of the life-giving tree,
4. When we look on the form that redeemed us, And His glory and majesty see,

As the numberless sand of the sea-shore, What a wonderful sight that will be!
Greeting there with a heavenly greeting, What a wonderful sight that will be!
Gazing out o'er the fair land of promise, What a wonderful sight that will be!
While as King of the saints He is reigning, What a wonderful sight that will be!

CHORUS.

Num-berless as the sand of the sea - - shore, Numberless
Numberless as the sand
as the sand of the shore; Oh, what a sight 'twill be,
as the sand of the shore;
When the ransomed host we see, As numberless as the sand of the sea-shore.

By permission. Copyright.

197. Our Loved Ones in Heaven.

Rev. J. W. Dadmun. Lesuer.

1. Come, all ye saints, to Pisgah's mountain, Come view our home beyond the tide;
2. There endless springs of life are flowing, There are the fields of living green;
3. Faith now beholds the flowing river, Coming from underneath the throne;

Hear now the voices of our loved ones, What they sing on the other side;
Mansions of beauty are provided, And the King of the saints is seen.
There, too, the Saviour reigns forever, And He'll welcome the faithful home.

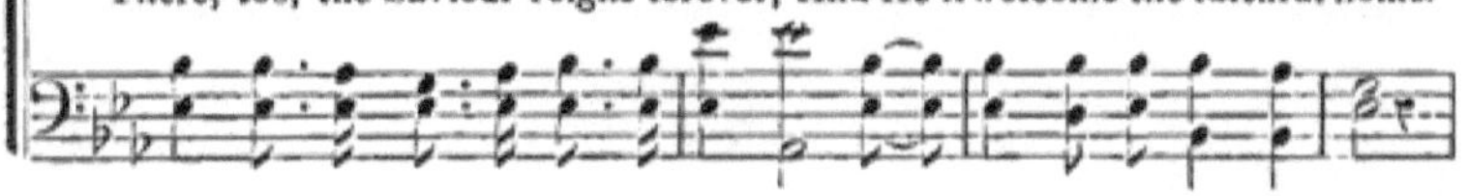

Some are singing of bright crowns of glory, Some of dear ones who stand near the [shore;
Soon my conflicts and toils will be ended; I shall join those who've passed on before;
Would you sit by the banks of the river With the friends you have loved by your [side?

CHORUS.
D.S.—O the prospect! it is so transporting, And no danger I fear from the tide;

For the fond heart must ever be clinging To the faithful we love evermore.
For my loved ones, O how I do miss them! I must press on and meet them once [more.
Would you join in the song of the angels? Then be ready to follow your Guide.

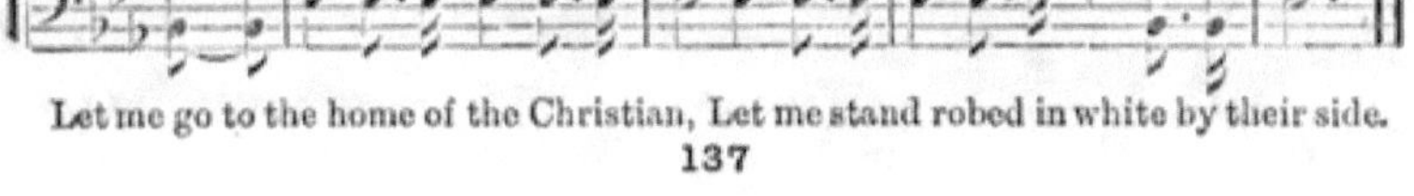

Let me go to the home of the Christian, Let me stand robed in white by their side.

198. That Beautiful World.

O. Snow. O. Snow.

1. There is a beautiful world, Where saints and angels sing;
A world where peace and pleasure reign, And heavenly praises ring.

2. There is a beautiful world, Where sorrow never comes;
A world where tears shall never fall In sighing for our home.

CHORUS.
We'll be there, we'll be there: Palms of victory, Crowns of glory, we shall wear In that beautiful world on high.

3 There is a beautiful world,
Unseen to mortal sight,
And darkness never enters there,
That home is fair and bright.

4 There is a beautiful world
Of harmony and love;
Oh, may we safely enter there,
And dwell with God above.

199. Sweet By and By.

S. F. Bennett. (G. H. 204. Key of G.)

1 There's a land that is fairer than day,
And by faith we can see it afar,
For the Father waits over the way,
To prepare us a dwelling place there.

Chorus.
‖: In the sweet by and by,
We shall meet on that beautiful shore. :‖

2 We shall sing on that beautiful shore
The melodious songs of the blest;
And our spirits shall sorrow no more—
Not a sigh for the blessing of rest.

3 To our bountiful Father above
We will offer the tribute of praise,
For the glorious gift of His love,
And the blessings that hallow our days.

4 We shall meet, we shall sing, we shall reign,
In the land where the saved never die;
We shall rest free from sorrow and pain,
Safe at home in the sweet by and by.

201. I'm Going Home.

Rev. Wm. Hunter. Dr. Wm. Miller. Arr.

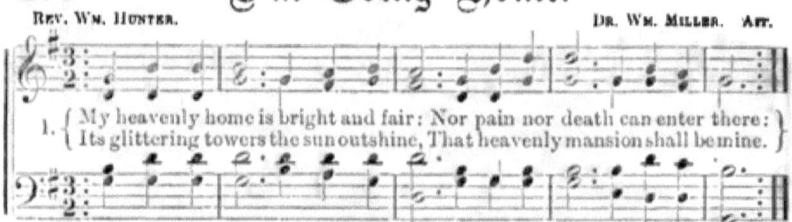

1. { My heavenly home is bright and fair: Nor pain nor death can enter there: }
   { Its glittering towers the sun outshine, That heavenly mansion shall be mine. }

CHORUS. { I'm going home, I'm going home, I'm going home to die no more: }
        { To die no more, to die no more, I'm going home to die no more. }

2 My Father's house is built on high,
  Far, far above the starry sky;
  When from this earthly prison free,
  That heavenly mansion mine shall be.
  I'm going home, etc.

3 Let others seek a home below,
  Which flames devour, or waves o'erflow;
  Be mine the happier lot to own
  A heavenly mansion near the throne.
  I'm going home, etc.

4 Then fail this earth, let stars decline,
  And sun and moon refuse to shine,
  All nature sink, and cease to be,
  That heavenly mansion stands for me.
  I'm going home, etc.

202. Beautiful River.

Rev. R. Lowry.   Rev. 22: 1.   Rev. R. Lowry, by per.

1. Shall we gather at the riv-er, Where bright angel feet have trod;
   With its crys-tal tide for-ev-er Flowing from the throne of God?
2. On the margin of the riv-er, Wash-ing up its sil-ver spray,
   We will walk and wor-ship ev-er, All the hap-py gold-en day.

CHORUS.
Yes, we'll gather at the riv-er, The beau-ti-ful, the beau-ti-ful riv-er—
Gather with the saints at the river That flows from the throne of God

3 Ere we reach the shining river,
  Lay we every burden down;
  Grace our spirits will deliver,
  And provide a robe and crown.

4 At the smiling of the river,
  Mirror of the Saviour's face,

  Saints whom death will never sever,
  Lift their songs of saving grace.

5 Soon we'll reach the shining river,
  Soon our pilgrimage will cease,
  Soon our happy hearts will quiver
  With the melody of peace.

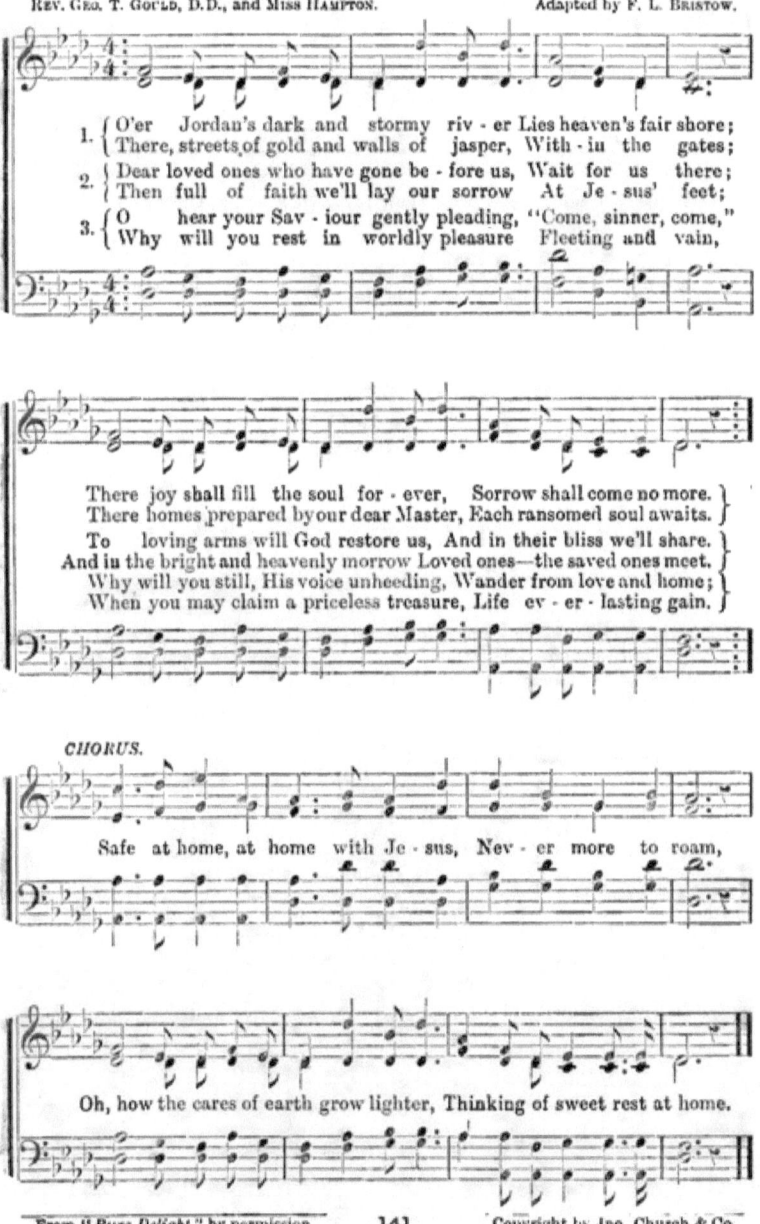

204. Calling Us Away.

I. WATTS.   "Here have we no continuing city."—*Heb.* 13:14.   Arranged.

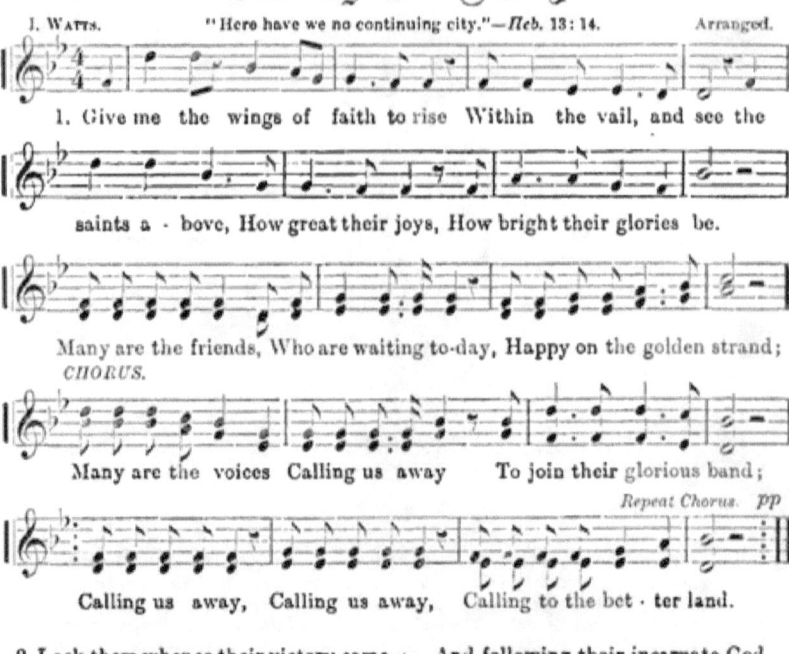

1. Give me the wings of faith to rise Within the vail, and see the saints a-bove, How great their joys, How bright their glories be. Many are the friends, Who are waiting to-day, Happy on the golden strand;

CHORUS.
Many are the voices Calling us away To join their glorious band;
Repeat Chorus. pp
Calling us away, Calling us away, Calling to the bet-ter land.

2 I ask them whence their victory came,
   They, with united breath,
Ascribe their conquest to the Lamb,
   Their triumph to His death.

3 They marked the footsteps that He trod,
   His zeal inspired their breast;

And following their incarnate God,
   Possess the promised rest.

4 Our glorious Leader claims our praise
   For His own pattern given;
While the long cloud of witnesses
   Shows the same path to heaven.

205. Triumph By and By.

DR. C. R. BLACKALL.   "I press towards the mark."—*Phil.* 3:14.   H. R. PALMER, by per.

1. The prize is set before us, To win, His words implore us, The eye of God is o'er us From on high, from on high; His loving tones are calling While sin is dark, appall-ing, 'Tis

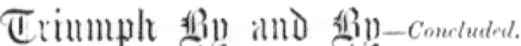

Triumph By and By—*Concluded.*

Je-sus gent-ly call-ing, He is nigh, He is nigh.

CHORUS.

By and by we shall meet Him, By and by we shall greet Him, And with

Jesus reign in glory, By and by, by and by; By and by we shall meet Him, By and

by we shall greet Him, And with Jesus reign in glo - ry, By and by.

2 We'll follow where He leadeth,
We'll pasture where He feedeth,
We'll yield to Him who pleadeth
  From on high, from on high;
Then naught from Him shall sever,
Our hope shall brighten ever,
And faith shall fail us never,
  He is nigh, He is nigh.

3 Our home is bright above us,
No trials dark to move us,
But Jesus dear to love us
  There on high, there on high;
We'll give Him best endeavor,
And praise His name forever,
His precious words can never,
  Never die, never die.

206   Over There.
(G. H. 92.)

1 Oh, think of the home over there,
  By the side of the river of light,
Where the saints, all immortal and fair,
  Are robed in their garments of white.
REFRAIN.
Over there, over there, etc.

2 Oh, think of the friends over there,
  Who before us the journey have trod,
Of the songs that they breathe on the air,
  In their home in the palace of God.

3 My Saviour is now over there,
  There my kindred and friends are at rest;
Then away from my sorrow and care,
  Let me fly to the land of the blest.

4 I'll soon be at home over there,
  For the end of my journey I see;
Many dear to my heart over there,
  Are watching and waiting for me.

207   Nearer My Home.
MISS P. CAREY.   (G. H. 192.)

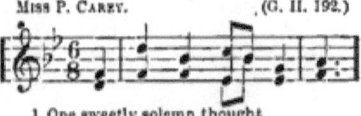

1 One sweetly solemn thought
  Comes to me o'er and o'er,
I'm nearer home to-day, to-day,
  Than I have been before.
CHORUS.
Nearer my home, nearer my home,
Nearer my home to-day, to-day,
Than I have been before.

2 Nearer my Father's house,
  Where many mansions be;
Nearer the great white throne to-day,
  Nearer the crystal sea.

3 Nearer the bound of life,
  Where burdens are laid down;
Nearer to leave the cross to-day,
  And nearer to the crown.

4 Be near me when my feet
  Are slipping o'er the brink;
For I am nearer home to-day,
  Perhaps, than now I think.

209 "The New Song."

H. POLLARD.   SOUTHERN MELODY.

CHORUS.
Wait a lit-tle while, Then we'll sing the New Song;
Wait a lit-tle while, Then we'll sing the New Song.

1. When the great Ju-bi-lee shall come, Then we'll sing the New Song;
   And Christ shall take His ransomed home, then we'll sing the New Song.

   End with Chorus.

2. When the glad shout shall rend the sky,
   Then we'll sing the New Song;
   "O grave, where is thy victory?"
   Then we'll sing the New Song.

3. When sorrow, pain, and death are o'er,
   Then we'll sing the New Song;
   And sighs and tears shall be no more,
   Then we'll sing the New Song.

4. When to the pearly gates we come,
   Then we'll sing the New Song;
   When we have reached our blissful home,
   Then we'll sing the New Song.

5. When we shall tread Life's river brink,
   Then we'll sing the New Song;
   And of those crystal waters drink,
   Then we'll sing the New Song.

6. Where all will be immortal, fair,
   There we'll sing the New Song;
   When blood-washed robes are ours to wear,
   Then we'll sing the New Song.

210 Shall We Meet.
TUNE: G. H. 199. KEY OF A.

1. Shall we meet beyond the river?
   Where the surges cease to roll?
   Where, in all the bright "forever,"
   Sorrow ne'er shall press the soul?

   CHORUS.
   Shall we meet? shall we meet?
   Shall we meet beyond the river?
   Shall we meet beyond the river,
   Where the surges cease to roll?

2. Shall we meet in that blest harbor,
   When the voyage of life is o'er?
   Shall we meet and cast the anchor
   By the fair celestial shore?

3. Shall we meet with many a loved one,
   That was torn from our embrace?
   Shall we listen to their voices,
   And behold them face to face?

4. Shall we meet with Christ our Saviour,
   When He comes to claim His own?
   Shall we know his blessed favour,
   And sit down upon His throne?

211 Till Jesus Comes.
TUNE: G. H. 304. KEY OF F.

1. Our souls are in His mighty hand,
   And He shall keep them still;
   And you and I shall surely stand
   With Him on Zion's hill.

   CHORUS.
   We'll work till Jesus comes,
   We'll work till Jesus comes,
   We'll work till Jesus comes,
   And we'll be gathered home.

2. Him eye to eye we there shall see;
   Our face like His shall shine:
   Oh! what a glorious company,
   When saints and angels join!

3. Oh! what a joyful meeting there!
   In robes of white arrayed,
   Palms in our hands we all shall bear,
   And crowns upon our head.

4. Then let us lawfully contend,
   And fight our passage through;
   Bear in our faithful minds the end,
   And keep the prize in view.

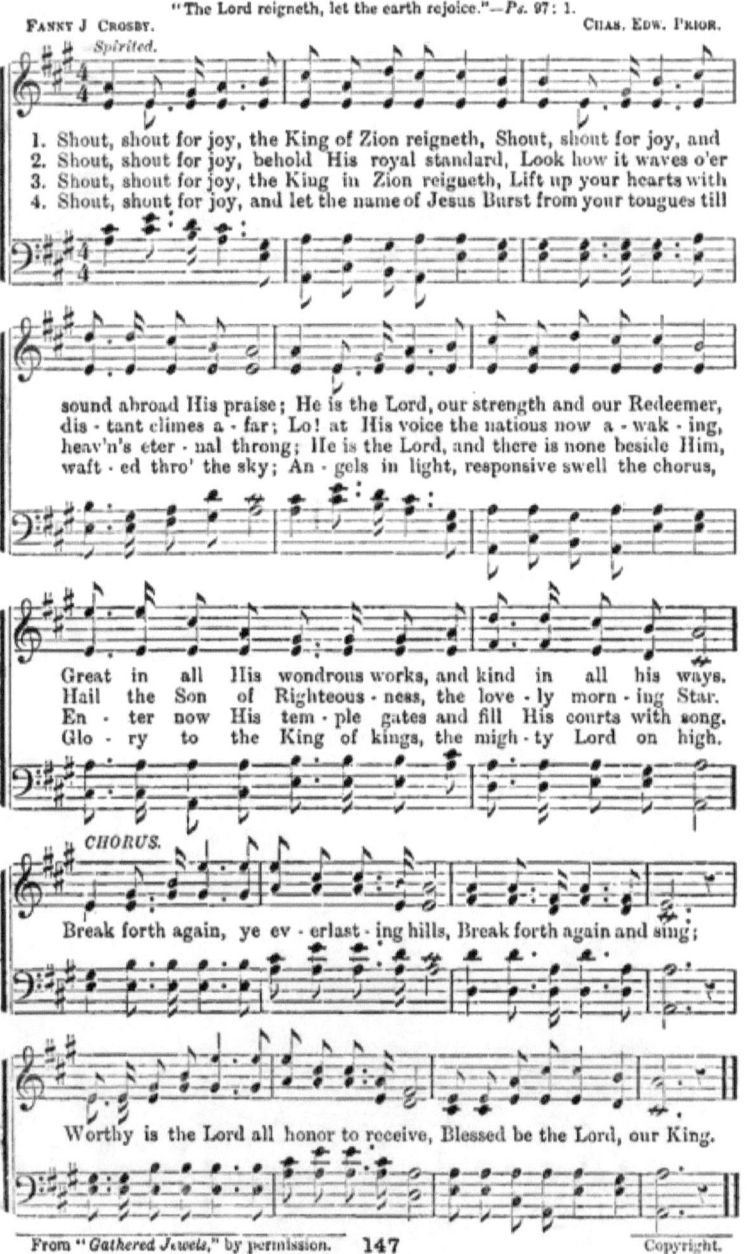

215 Why Not To-Night?

TUNE: No. 144.

1 Oh, do not let the word depart,
  And close thine eyes against the light;
  Poor sinner, harden not thy heart;
  Thou would'st be saved—why not to-night?

CHORUS.

Why not to-night? why not to-night?
Thou would'st be saved—why not to-night?

2 To-morrow's sun may never rise
  To bless thy long-deluded sight;
  This is the time, oh, then, be wise;
  Thou would'st be saved—why not to-night?

3 Our God in pity lingers still,
  And wilt thou thus His love requite.
  Renounce at once thy stubborn will;
  Thou would'st be saved—why not to-night?

4 Our blessed Lord refuses none
  Who would to Him their souls unite;
  Bel'eve on Him—the work is done;
  Thou would'st be saved—why not to-night?

216 Where is My Boy To-Night?

DR. R. LOWRY. (G. H. 279.)

1 Where is my wandering boy to-night?
  The boy of my tenderest care,
  The boy that was once my joy and light,
  The child of my love and prayer?

CHORUS.

O where is my boy to-night?
O where is my boy to-night? [knows,
My heart o'erflows, for I love him he
O where is my boy to-night?

2 Once he was pure as morning dew,
  As he knelt at his mother's knee;
  No face was so bright, no heart more true
  And none was so sweet as he.

3 O could I see you now, my boy,
  As fair as in olden time,
  When prattle and smile made home a joy,
  And life was a merry chime!

4 Go for my wandering boy to-night;
  Go, search for him where you will;
  But bring him to me with all his blight,
  And tell him I love him still.

217 Heaven My Home.

MISS M. HAMPTON.

TUNE: "Home, Sweet Home." KEY OF E FLAT.

1 A pilgrim I journey o'er life's rugged way,
  And know I am nearing my home day by day;
  Tho' storm-clouds may gather, no evil I'll fear,
  My Saviour is with me to comfort and cheer.

CHORUS.

Home, home, sweet, sweet home,
Oh, the joy of the meeting with loved ones
    at home.

2 When burdened and weary I faint by the way,
  His strong hand supports me, His staff is my stay;
  My burden grows lighter, I rise and rejoice
  At the touch of His hand and the sound of His voice.

3 My journey grows shorter, I soon shall behold
  The beautiful gates of the city of gold,
  And through their bright portals with rapture I'll see
  The mansion prepared by my Saviour for me.

4 Oh, what are my conflicts, my trials and tears?
  They'll all be forgotten when heaven appears;
  Oh, glorious prospect! no more I shall roam,
  But dwell evermore with my Saviour at home.

218 The Precious Name.

MRS. BAXTER. (G. H. 72.)

1 Take the Name of Jesus with you,
  Child of sorrow and of woe—
  It will joy and comfort give you,
  Take it, then, where'er you go.

CHORUS.

Precious Name, O how sweet!
Hope of earth and joy of heaven.

2 Take the Name of Jesus ever
  As a shield from every snare;
  If temptations round you gather,
  Breathe that Holy Name in prayer.

3 Oh! the precious Name of Jesus;
  How it thrills our souls with joy,
  When His loving arms receive us,
  And His songs our tongues employ!

4 At the Name of Jesus bowing,
  Falling prostrate at His feet,
  King of kings in heaven we'll crown Him,
  When our journey is complete.

219 In the Cross of Christ I Glory.

Sir J. Bowring.   J. Conkey.

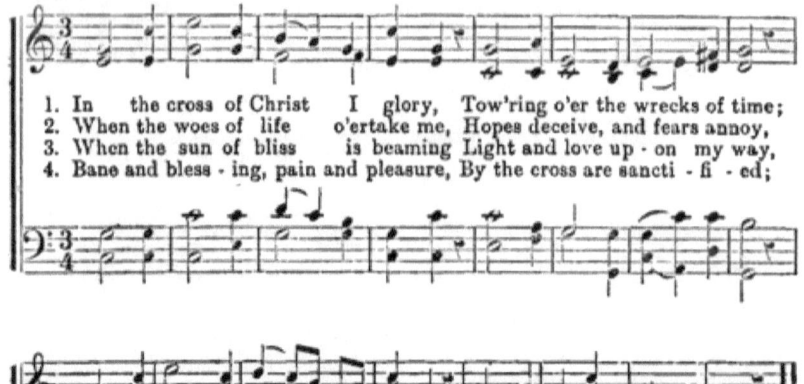

1. In the cross of Christ I glory, Tow'ring o'er the wrecks of time;
2. When the woes of life o'ertake me, Hopes deceive, and fears annoy,
3. When the sun of bliss is beaming Light and love up-on my way,
4. Bane and bless-ing, pain and pleasure, By the cross are sancti-fi-ed;

All the light of sa-cred sto-ry Gathers round its head sublime.
Nev-er shall the cross for-sake me; Lo! it glows with peace and joy.
From the cross the ra-diance streaming Adds more lustre to the day.
Peace is there, that knows no measure, Joys that through all time abide.

220 There's a Wideness in God's Mercy.

F. W. Faber.   Tune: No. 219.

1 There's a wideness in God's mercy,
   Like the wideness of the sea:
There's a kindness in His justice,
   Which is more than liberty.

2 There is welcome for the sinner,
   And more graces for the good;
There is mercy with the Saviour;
   There is healing in His blood.

3 For the love of God is broader
   Than the measure of man's mind;
And the heart of the Eternal
   Is most wonderfully kind.

4 If our love were but more simple,
   We should take Him at His word;
And our lives would be all sunshine
   In the sweetness of our Lord.

221 Come, Thou Long Expected Jesus.

C. Wesley.   Tune: No. 219.

1 Come, thou long expected Jesus,
   Born to set Thy people free;
From our fears and sins release us,
   Let us find our rest in Thee.

2 Israel's strength and consolation,
   Hope of all the earth Thou art;
Blest desire of every nation,
   Joy of every trusting heart.

3 Born Thy people to deliver,
   Born a child and yet a King,
Born to reign in us forever,
   Now Thy gracious kingdom bring.

4 By Thine own eternal Spirit,
   Rule in all our hearts alone;
By Thine all-sufficient merit,
   Raise us to Thy glorious throne.

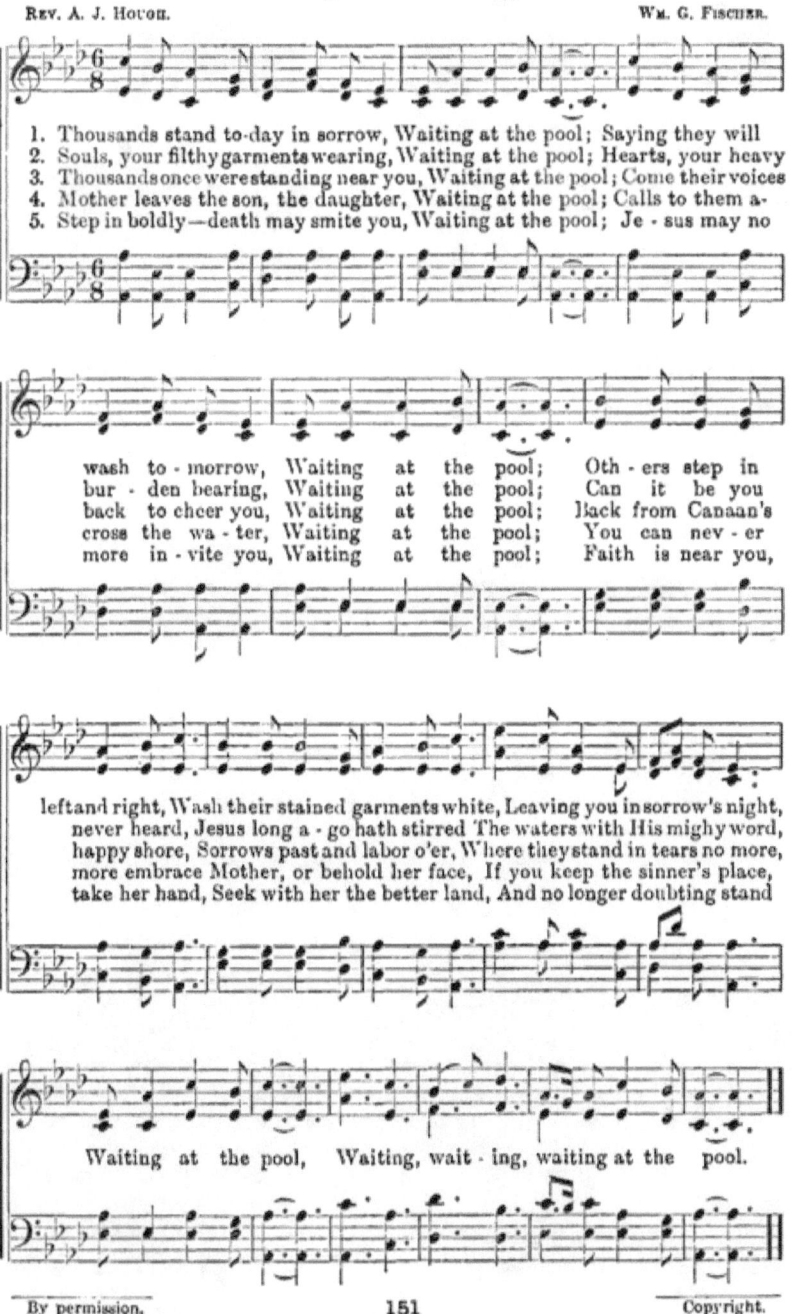

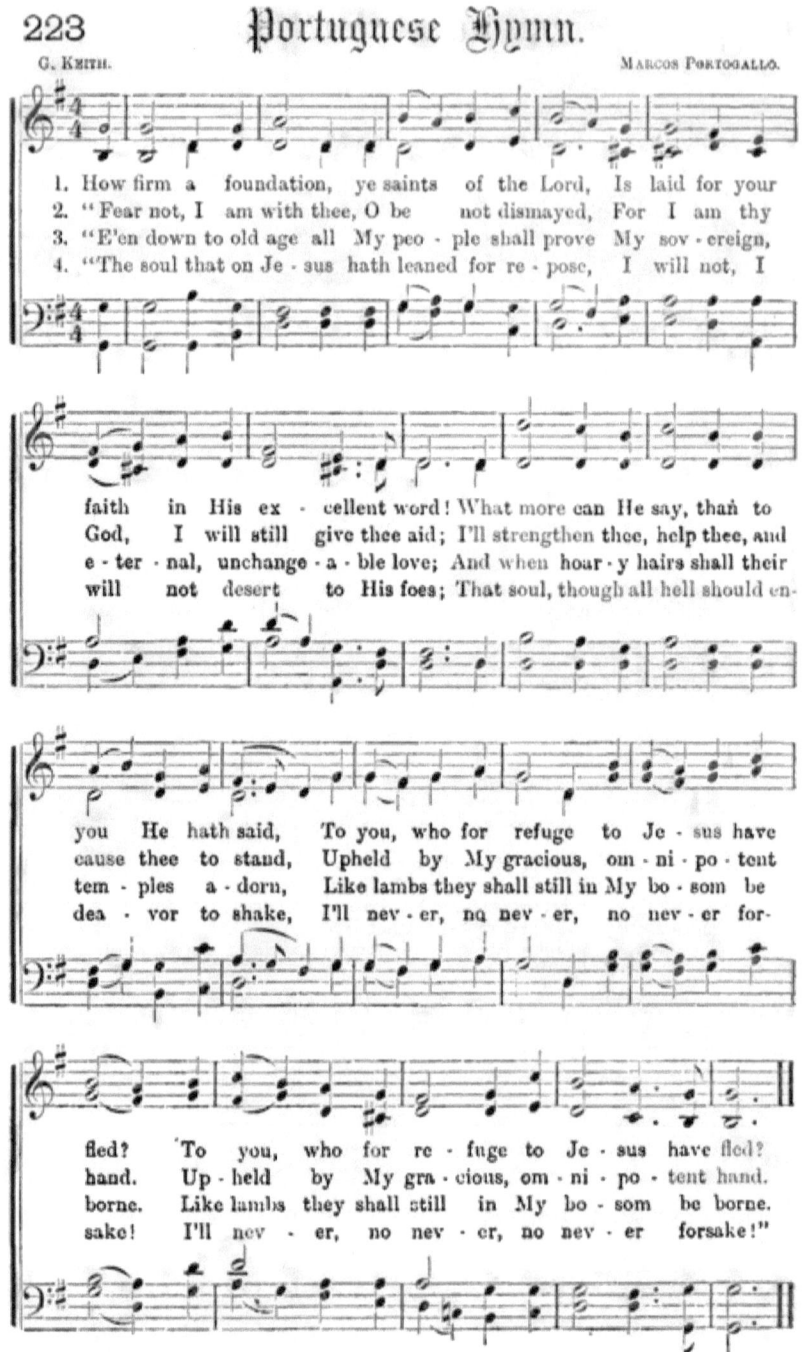

224 O Weep for the Fallen.

Arranged.   TUNE: No. 223.

1 O weep for the fallen, hang your head in sorrow,
And mournfully sing the requiem, sad and slow;
Thousands have perished by the fell destroyer,
‖:O weep for youth and beauty :‖ in the grave laid low.

2 Sad voices of wailing tell of hopeless anguish,
While sorrowing mothers bid us onward go;
Hark to their accents, there's the broken-hearted,
‖: Who weep for youth and beauty :‖ in the grave laid low.

3 O hear how they bid us sound the timely warning,
While yet there is hope to shun the cup of woe;
For, is it nothing, ye who see no danger,
‖:To weep for youth and beauty :‖ in the grave laid low?

4 Then weep for the fallen, but, amid your sorrow,
Still point them to Christ Who freedom can bestow;
Rescue the nation from the fell destroyer,
‖: For why should youth and beauty :‖ in the grave lie low.

225 The Three Warnings.

"Resist not, Grieve not, Quench not."

P. P. BLISS.   TUNE: 223.

1 The Spirit, oh, sinner,
In mercy doth move,
Thy heart, so long hardened,
Of sin to reprove;
Resist not the Spirit,
Nor longer delay;
‖: God's gracious entreaties
May end with to-day. :‖

2 Oh, child of the kingdom,
From sin service cease:
Be filled with the Spirit,
With comfort and peace.
Oh, grieve not the Spirit,
Thy Teacher is He,
‖: That Jesus, thy Saviour,
May glorified be. :‖

3 Defiled is the temple,
Its beauty laid low,
On God's holy altar
The embers faint glow.
By love yet rekindled,
A flame may be fanned;
‖: Oh, quench not the Spirit,
The Lord is at hand! :‖

226 Adeste Fideles.

TUNE: No. 223.

1 O come, all ye faithful, enter now the temple,
Which here our great God has made for all who Him serve;
Raise we our voices, joyful in thanksgiving,
‖:With cheerful adoration :‖ thus praise we the Lord.

2 Come, let us worship our dear Lord and Saviour,
Who gave His precious self the sinner to save;
Grateful devotion offer we unto Him,
‖: With cheerful adoration :‖ thus praise we the Lord.

3 Ever sincerely offering our homage
To our benign, forgiving Lord and God;
Bless Him forever, sing His praise eternally,
‖: With cheerful adoration :‖ thus praise we the Lord.

4 Glorious, eternal, merciful Redeemer,
Deign to receive our earnest fervent prayers:
Graciously hear us, bending thus before Thee,
‖: With cheerful adoration :‖ thus praise we the Lord.

227 Don't Go Near the Bar-Room.

KEY OF B FLAT.

TUNE: "Just before the Battle."

1 Don't go near the bar-room, brother,
Listen to a sister's prayer,
Do not yield to its temptation,—
Sin and death are lurking there.
Do not heed the gilded palace,
'Tis a mask the tempter wears,
For deep destruction lurks beneath it,
And will meet you unawares.

CHORUS.

Dearest brother, will you never
From the luring wine abstain,
O by the love you bear me, brother,
Break, O break the demon's chain.

2 Don't go near the bar-room, brother,
Shun it as an evil place;
It will bring you desolation,—
Cover you with deep disgrace.
Friends and kindred all around you,
Counsel you to pass it by;
The pleadings of your darling sister
Strengthen you once more to try.

3 Don't go near the bar-room, brother,
Touch not, taste not of the wine,
There is poison in its contact,—
Do not worship at its shrine.
Join the grand teetotal army,
Shun the bar-room and the cup,
Then in strong love we'll work together,
Till the demon shall give up.

228. Oh, Sing to Me of Heaven.

1. Oh, sing to me of heaven When I'm about to die,
2. When the last moment comes, Oh, watch my dying face,
3. Then to my raptured soul Let one sweet song be given,
4. Then close my sightless eyes, And lay me down to rest,
5. Then, round my senseless clay, Assemble those I love,

CHORUS.
There'll be no sorrow there, There'll be no sorrow there,

Sing songs of holy ecstasy, To waft my soul on high!
To catch the bright seraphic gleam Which o'er my features plays.
Let music cheer me last on earth, And greet me first in heaven.
And fold my pale and icy hands Upon my lifeless breast.
And sing of heaven, delightful heaven, My glorious home above.

In heaven above, where all is love, There'll be no sorrow there.

229. I'm Glad Salvation's Free.

C. WESLEY.   TUNE: No. 223.

1 When shall Thy love constrain,
   And force me to Thy breast?
   When shall my soul return again
   To her eternal rest?

CHORUS.
‖: I'm glad salvation's free, :‖
Salvation's free for you and me,
I'm glad salvation's free.

2 Ah! what avails my strife,
   My wandering to and fro?
   Thou hast the words of endless life:
   Ah! whither should I go?

3 And can I yet delay
   My little all to give?
   To tear my soul from earth away,
   For Jesus to receive?

4 Nay, but I yield, I yield;
   I can hold out no more;
   I sink, by dying love compelled,
   And own Thee conqueror.

230. I Love to Think of Heaven.

TUNE: No. 228.

1 I love to think of heaven,
   Where white-robed angels are,
   Where many a friend is gathered safe,
   From fear, and toil, and care.

CHORUS.
‖: There'll be no parting there, :‖
In heaven above where all is love,
There'll be no parting there.

2 I love to think of heaven,
   Where my Redeemer reigns,
   Where rapturous songs of triumph rise,
   In endless, joyous strains.

3 I love to think of heaven,
   The saints' eternal home,
   Where palms, and robes, and crowns ne'[fade,
   And all our joys are one.

4 I love to think of heaven,
   The greetings there we'll meet,
   The harps—the songs forever ours—
   The walks—the golden streets.

231 Beautiful Words.
(G. H. 282.)

1 Sing them over again to me,
   Wonderful words of Life,
   Let me more of their beauty see,
   Wonderful words of Life.
   Words of life and beauty,
   Teach me faith and duty;
   ‖: Beautiful words, wonderful words,
   Wonderful words of Life. :‖

2 Christ, the blessed One, gives to all
   Wonderful words of Life;
   Sinner, list to the loving call,
   Wonderful words of Life.
   All so freely given,
   Wooing us to heaven,
   Beautiful, etc.

3 Sweetly echo the Gospel call,
   Wonderful words of Life;
   Offer pardon and peace to all,
   Wonderful words of Life.
   Jesus, only Saviour,
   Sanctify forever,
   Beautiful, etc.

232 Come We.
Tune: No. 228.

1 Come we that love the Lord,
   And let our joys be known;
   Join in a song with sweet accord,
   And thus surround His throne.

Cho.—‖: I'm glad salvation's free, :‖
   Salvation's free for you and me,
   I'm glad salvation's free.

2 Let those refuse to sing,
   Who never knew our God;
   But servants of the Heavenly King
   May speak their joys abroad.

3 There we shall see His face,
   And never, never sin;
   There, from the rivers of His grace,
   Drink endless pleasures in.

4 Yes, and before we rise
   To that immortal state,
   The thoughts of such amazing bliss
   Should constant joys create.

5 Then let our songs abound,
   And every tear be dry;
   We're marching through Immanuel's
   ground
   To fairer worlds on high.

233 Speaking for Jesus.
F. J. Crosby.

1 Now just a word for Jesus,
   Your dearest Friend so true;
   Come, cheer our hearts, and tell us,
   What He has done for you.

2 Now just a word for Jesus—
   'Twill help us on our way;
   One little word for Jesus,
   Oh speak, or sing, or pray.

3 Now just a word for Jesus;
   You feel your sins forgiven,
   And by His grace are striving
   To reach a home in heaven.

234 Have You Been to Jesus?

1 Have you been to Jesus for the cleansing power?   [Lamb?
   Are you washed in the blood of the
   Are you fully trusting in His grace this hour?   [Lamb?
   Are you wash'd in the blood of the

Cho.—Are you wash'd in the blood,
   In the soul-cleansing blood of the Lamb?
   Are your garments spotless?
   Are they white as snow?
   Are you wash'd in the blood of the Lamb?

2 Are you walking daily by the Saviour's side?   [Lamb?
   Are you wash'd in the blood of the
   Do you rest each moment in the crucified?   [Lamb?
   Are you wash'd in the blood of the

3 When the Bridegroom cometh will your robes be white,   [Lamb?
   Pure and white in the blood of the
   Will your soul be ready for the mansions bright?   [Lamb?
   And be wash'd in the blood of the

4 Lay aside the garments that are stained with sin,   [Lamb;
   And be wash'd in the blood of the
   There's a fountain flowing for the soul unclean—
   O be wash'd in the blood of the Lamb!

235. God is Calling Yet.

GERHARD TERSTEGEN.
E. O. EXCELL.

1. God call-ing yet! shall I not hear? Earth's pleasures shall I still hold dear? Shall life's swift passing years all fly, And still my soul in slumber lie?
2. God call-ing yet! shall I not rise? Can I His loving voice despise, And basely His kind care repay? He calls me still; can I delay?
3. God call-ing yet! and shall He knock, And I my heart the closer lock? He still is waiting to receive, And shall I dare His Spirit grieve?
4. God call-ing yet! and shall I give No heed, but still in bondage live? I wait, but He does not forsake; He calls me still; my heart awake!
5. God call-ing yet! I cannot stay; My heart I yield with out delay: Vain world, farewell, from thee I part; The voice of God has reached my heart.

CHORUS.

Call - - ing, Call - - ing,
God is calling yet, oh, hear Him, God is calling yet, oh, hear Him, God is

From "*Great Awakening*," by permission.
Copyright 1886, by Dr. Wm. Briggs.

238 God is Love.

Arranged.   Arr. by H. T. C. & W. J. B.

3 We'll tell to earth's remotest bounds,
   God is love, God is love,
In Christ we have redemption found,
   God is love, God is love.
He is our Sun and Shield by day,
By night He near our tents will stay,
He will be with us all the way,
   God is love, God is love.

4 When by His grace our race is run,
   God is love, God is love,
The battle fought, the victory won,
   God is love, God is love,
Then with united voice we'll sing
The praises of our Saviour King, [ring,
Through heaven the glad refrain shall
   God is love, God is love.

239 The Name of Jesus.

C. WESLEY. Arranged.   TUNE: No. 237.

1 O for a thousand tongues to sing
   My great Redeemer's praise!
The glories of my God and King,
   The triumphs of His grace!

CHORUS.

It was Christ, it was Christ, who first
   gave me the light
And the burden of my heart rolled
   away,   [sight,
When I came by faith I received my
And now I am happy all the day.

2 Jesus! the Name that charms our
   fears,
   That bids our sorrows cease,

'Tis music in the sinner's ears,
   'Tis life, and health, and peace.

3 He breaks the power of cancelled sin,
   He sets the prisoner free;
His blood can make the foulest clean,
   His blood availed for me.

4 He speaks, and, listening to His voice,
   New life the dead receive;
The mournful, broken hearts rejoice,
   The humble poor believe.

5 See all your sins on Jesus laid:
   The Lamb of God was slain,
His soul was once an offering made
   For every soul of man.

Hallelujah for the Cross! — *Concluded.*

lu - jah! Hal - le - lu - - - jah for the
hal - le - lu - jah! hal - le - lu - jah for the cross! halle-

cross! Hal - le - lu - jah! hal - le
lu - jah for the cross! Hal - le - lu - jah!

lu - jah! It shall never suffer loss;
hal - le - lu - jah! It shall never suffer, never suffer loss;

Hal - le - lu - jah! hal - le - lu - jah! hal - le - lu - jah for the

cross! Hal - le - lu - jah! hal - le - lu - jah! It shall never suffer loss.

241 I Am So Glad.

(G. H. 23.)

1 I am so glad that our Father in Heaven
Tells of His love in the book He has given;
Wonderful things in the Bible I see;
This is the dearest, that Jesus loves me.

CHORUS.

I am so glad that Jesus loves me,
Jesus loves me, Jesus loves me;
I am so glad that Jesus loves me,
Jesus loves even me.

2 Though I forget Him and wander away,
Still he doth love me wherever I stray;
Back to His dear loving arms would I flee,
When I remember that Jesus loves me.

3 Jesus loves me, and I know I love Him,
Love brought Him down my poor soul to redeem!
Yes, it was love made Him die on the tree;
Oh, I am certain that Jesus loves me.

4 If one should ask of me, how could I tell?
Glory to Jesus, I know very well;
God's Holy Spirit with mine doth agree,
Constantly witnessing—Jesus loves me.

5 In this assurance I find sweetest rest,
Trusting in Jesus I know I am blest;
Satan, dismayed, from my soul now doth flee,
When I just tell him that Jesus loves me.

242 Ring the Bells.

REV. W. O. CUSHING.   (G. H. 19.)

1 Ring the bells of heaven! there is joy to-day,
For a soul returning from the wild;
See! the Father meets him out upon the way,
Welcoming His weary, wandering child.

CHORUS.

Glory! glory! how the angels sing;
Glory! glory! how the loud harps ring;
'Tis the ransomed army, like a mighty sea,
Pealing forth the anthem of the free.

2 Ring the bells of heaven! there is joy to-day,
For the wanderer now is reconciled;
Yes, a soul is rescued from his sinful way,
And is born anew a ransomed child.

3 Ring the bells of heaven! spread the feast to-day,
Angels swell the glad triumphant strain!
Tell the joyous tidings! bear it far away,
For a precious soul is born again

243 Angels Hovering Round.

1 There are angels hovering round,
There are angels hovering round,
There are |: angels :|| hovering round.

2 |: To carry the tidings home, :|

3 |: To the new Jerusalem, :|

4 |: Poor sinners are coming home, :|

5 |: And Jesus bids them come, :|

6 |: Let Him that heareth come, :|

7 |: Whosoever will may come, :|

8 |: O, come and trust Him now, :|

9 |: Now praise we all our God, :|

10 |: For His redeeming love. :|

244 Come.

MRS. JOHNSON.   (G. H. 309.)

1 Oh word, of words the sweetest,
Oh word, in which there lie
All promise, all fulfilment,
And end of mystery!
Lamenting or rejoicing,
With doubt or terror nigh,
I hear the "Come!" of Jesus,
And to His cross I fly.

CHORUS.

"Come! oh, come to Me!
"Come! oh, come to Me!
"Weary, heavy-laden,
"Come! oh, come to Me!"

2 O soul! why shouldst thou wander
From such a loving Friend?
Cling closer, closer to Him,
Stay with Him to the end.
Alas! I am so helpless,
So very full of sin,
For I am ever wandering,
And coming back again.

3 Oh, each time draw me nearer,
That soon the "Come!" may be
Nought but a gentle whisper
To one close, close to Thee;
Then, over sea and mountain,
Far from or near my home,
I'll take Thy hand and follow,
At that sweet whisper, "Come!"

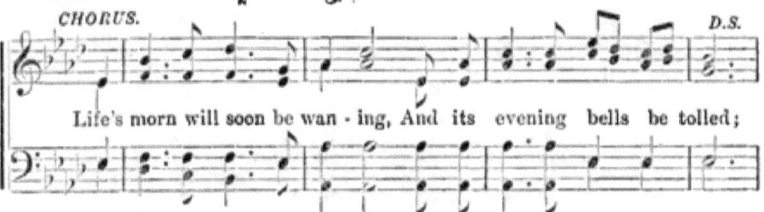

247. Motto Song.

This concert exercise will, when properly given, be found to carry off the palm at Sunday School Anniversaries. It is to be sung by nine girls, not too small, each turning to view an appropriate letter as her verse is sung. It is well to have this song as the closing piece.—H. T. C.

T. W. HUGHES. P. P. BLISS, by per.

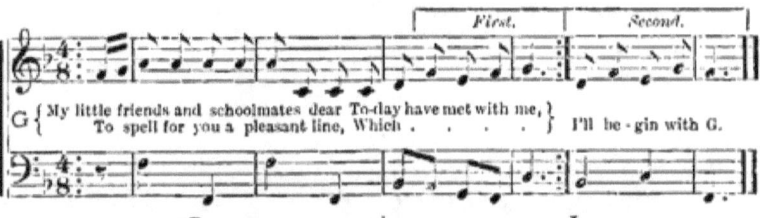

G
My little friends and schoolmates dear
 To-day have met with me,
To spell for you a pleasant line,
 Which I'll begin with G.

O
And I will do my little mite
 The precious words to show;
And for this worthy purpose, I
 Will lend my great, round O.

D
My letter ends the holy name
 Of Him we love and fear;
'Tis D—I'll turn it round to view,
 And you will see it here.

I
My mission is an humble one,
 Yet to do good I'll try;
To help all, when I'm needed, so
 I now will furnish I.

S
My little aid is needed now,
 To give this song success;
So joyfully I bring to view
 My crooked letter S.

L
And now another word we spell—
 A word endeared to all;
And as I see my turn has come,
 The letter L I'll call.

O
Although my letter you have seen
 Upon the platform here,
Still our sweet word, without an O,
 You could not tell, I fear.

V
As no one in our little band
 Has brought the letter V,
I hope it will not come amiss
 If now supplied by me.

E
This and the following verse to tune No. 95.
I will close the joyful tidings—
 Soon our motto you will see;
All can read it very plainly
 When I add the letter E.

ALL.
God is love—His mercy brightens
 All the path in which we rove,
Bliss He wakes and woe He lightens:
 God is wisdom—God is love.

249. Responsive Service.

Arranged by H. T. CROSSLEY.

Leader.—"The Lord is nigh unto all them that call upon Him, to all that call upon Him in truth."—(*Ps.* 145 : 18.)

Congregation.—"If we confess our sins, He is faithful and just to forgive us our sins, and to cleanse us from all unrighteousness."
—(1 *Jno.* 1 : 9.)

Leader.—"He that hath received His testimony hath set to his seal that God is true."
—(*Jno.* 3 : 33.)

All sing.

BRADBURY. (No. 101.)

Just as I am, without one plea,
But that Thy blood was shed for me,
And that Thou bidd'st me come to Thee,
O Lamb of God! I come, I come!

Leader.—"Examine yourselves, whether ye be in the faith."—(2 *Cor.* 13 : 5.)

Congregation.—"Being justified by faith, we have peace with God through our Lord Jesus Christ."—(*Rom.* 5 : 1.)

Leader.—"The Lord of peace Himself give you peace always by all means."—(2 *Thess.* 3 : 16.)

Congregation.—"Thou wilt keep him in perfect peace, whose mind is stayed on Thee; because he trusteth in Thee. Trust ye in the Lord forever; for in the Lord Jehovah is everlasting strength."
—(*Is.* 26 : 3, 4.)

All sing.

I HAVE A SAVIOUR. (G.H. 11.)

I have a peace: it is calm as a river—
A peace that the friends of this world never knew;
My Saviour alone is its Author and Giver,
And oh, could I know it was given to you.
‖: For you I am praying, :‖ I'm praying for you.

Leader.—"He is able to succor them that are tempted."—(*Heb.* 2 : 18.)

Congregation.—"I know whom I have believed, and am persuaded that He is able to keep that which I have committed unto Him against that day."—(2 *Tim.* 1 : 12.)

Leader.—"God is able to make *all* grace abound toward you; that ye, *always* having *all* sufficiency in *all* things, may abound to *every* good work."—(2 *Cor.* 9 : 8.)

Congregation.—"Unto Him that is able to do exceeding abundantly above all that we ask or think, according to the power that worketh in us, unto Him be glory."—(*Eph.* 3 : 20, 21.)

All sing.

IT IS WELL. (No. 152.)

Though Satan should buffet, though trials should come,
Let this blest assurance control,
That Christ hath regarded my helpless estate,
And hath shed His own blood for my soul.
It is well with my soul,
‖: It is well :‖ with my soul.

Leader.—Our Lord says, "I will make an everlasting covenant with you."—(*Is.* 55 : 3.)

Congregation.—"Come and let us join ourselves to the Lord in a perpetual covenant that shall not be forgotten."—(*Jer.* 50 : 5.)

Leader.—"There remaineth . . . . a rest to the people of God."—(*Heb.* 4 : 9.)

Congregation.—"Now unto Him that is able to keep" *us* "from falling, and to present" *us* "faultless before the presence of His glory with exceeding joy, to the only wise God our Saviour, be glory and majesty, dominion and power, both now and ever. Amen." (*Jude* 24.)

All sing.

SWEET BY AND BY. (G.H. 204.)

We shall meet, we shall sing, we shall reign,
In the land where the saved never die;
We shall rest free from sorrow and pain,
Safe at home in the sweet by and by.

250 Scripture Passages

FOR

INQUIRY ROOM AND HOME.

SELECTED BY H. T. CROSSLEY.

FOR THE UNCONVERTED.

1. Are you willing to be a Christian?
   Rev. 3:20; *Jer.* 29:13; 1 *Jno.* 1:9; *Jno.* 12:32; *Is.* 45:22; *Jno.* 3:14-18.
2. Are you neglecting, halting, or resisting?
   Heb. 2:1-3; *Heb.* 3:7-11; 1 *Kings* 18:21; *Prov.* 29:1; 2 *Cor.* 6:2.
3. Are you ashamed to confess Christ?
   Matt. 10:32, 33; *Luke* 9:26; *Ps.* 25:23; *Rom.* 1:16; *Rom.* 10:8-11.
4. Are you trusting in your morality, or church membership?
   Jer. 17:9, 10; *Rom.* 3:20-23; *Jno.* 16:8, 9; *Jno.* 5:10-13.
5. Do you say: "I'm too great a sinner?"
   Is. 1:18; *Is.* 43:25; *Is.* 55:6, 7; 1 *Tim.* 1:15; *Heb.* 7:23; *Rev.* 22:17.
6. Are you afraid you will not find?
   Jer. 29:13; *Matt.* 7:7, 8; *Matt.* 11:28, 29; *Is.* 45:19, 22; *Jno.* 7:17.
7. Do you fear you'll fall away?—Can't God keep you?
   1 *Cor.* 10:13; 2 *Cor.* 12:9; *Rom.* 8:35-39; *Rom.* 14:4; 1 *Peter* 1:5; 2 *Tim.* 1:12; *Jude* 24, 25.
8. Have you harsh views of God?
   Jno. 3:16; *Matt.* 7:9-11; 1 *Jno.* 3:16; *Jno.* 4:7-10, 16, 19; *Rom.* 5:6-8.
   Do not discriminate between Jesus and God the Father.
   Jno. 14:8, 9; 1 *Tim.* 3:16; 2 *Cor.* 5:18-21; *Ps.* 9:10.
9. Are you a scorner, or an honest doubter?
   Jno. 7:17; *Jno.* 3:19, 21; *Jno.* 10:15, 18, 30; *Acts* 17:11, 12; *Prov.* 1:20-23.
10. Do inconsistencies of others hinder you?
    Josh. 24:15; *Phil.* 4:8; *Jno.* 6:66-69; *Rom.* 14:12; *Jno.* 21:21, 22.
11. Does worldly pleasure, honor, or business prevent you?
    Matt. 6:33; *Matt.* 19:29, 30; *Mark* 8:36, 37; 2 *Cor.* 8:9; 1 *Tim.* 4:8.
12. Do you say: "I don't feel enough?"
    Ps. 32:9; *Matt.* 12:19-21; *Eph.* 5:14; *Jno.* 12:32; *Is.* 1:3; *Ps.* 95:6-11.
13. Do you think it hard to live a Christian?
    Micah 6:8; 1 *Jno.* 5:3-5; *Jno.* 15:15; 2 *Cor.* 9:8.
14. Are you a backslider? Return now.
    Rev. 2:5; *Hos.* 14:4; *Jer.* 2:19; *Jer.* 3:11-14, 22; *Luke* 15:18-24.
15. Are you living in open or secret sin?
    Eccl. 8:11; *Eccl.* 9:18; *Eccl.* 11:9; *Gal.* 6:7, 8; *Prov.* 11:19; *Prov.* 28:13; *Is.* 55:6, 7.

FOR CHRISTIANS.

1. Is your heart filled with love?
   1 *Jno.* 4:16-19; *Mark* 12:29-31; *Eph.* 3:17-21; *Jno.* 14:23; *Rev.* 3:20.
2. Are you doing your duty to the poor?
   Ps. 41:1-3; *Prov.* 19:17; 1 *Tim.* 6:17-19; *Matt.* 25:31-46.
3. Do not expect similar manifestations and details in all conversions and Christian experiences. The yielding trust and peace are the essentials.
   Acts 8:26-39; *Acts* 9:1-22; *Acts* 10:42-48; *Acts* 16:14, 15; *Acts* 25:34; *Heb.* 10:23; *Heb.* 12:12; *Rom.* 5:1; *Is.* 26:3, 4.
4. Can we be certain we are saved?
   Matt. 24:44; 1 *Cor.* 2:12; *Heb.* 6:16-20; 1 *Jno.* 3:1, 2; *Jno.* 10:2-5, 14.
5. How may we know we are Christians?
   Rom. 5:1; *Rom.* 8:14-17; 1 *Jno.* 2:3; 1 *Jno.* 3:14, 24; 1 *Jno.* 5:9-12; *Jno.* 3:33.
6. Have your fears of death? Read:
   Ps. 23:4; *Josh.* 3:14-17; *Josh.* 4:1-18; *Heb.* 2:14, 15; 1 *Cor.* 15:55-58.
7. Have you doubts about reaching heaven?
   Lu. 12:32; *Heb.* 6:16-20; 2 *Tim.* 1:12; *Jude* 24, 25.

FOR CHRISTIAN WORKERS.

1. There is a power that qualifies and disposes for work. Have you received this power?
   Acts 1:8; *Is.* 6:5-8; *Ps.* 51:9-13; *Lu.* 24:48, 49.
2. Have faith in God to direct and use you, though weak.
   1 *Cor.* 1:27-31; 1 *Cor.* 3:6-9; *Acts* 8:29; *Dan.* 12:3; *Ps.* 126:6; *Jas.* 5:19, 20.
3. Have unbounded faith that children and youth can be Christians.
   Prov. 22:6; *Matt.* 18:1-6; *Mark* 10:13-16; *Eccl.* 12:1; *Jno.* 21:15.
4. Do not argue, but invite to prove.
   Jno. 1:45, 46; *Is.* 1:18; *Is.* 55:6, 7; 1 *Thess.* 5:21; 1 *Tim.* 1:15.
5. Use God's Word and Christian experience.
   Jer. 20:9; *Jno.* 1:41, 45; *Acts* 8:35; *Acts* 26:9-27; 2 *Tim.* 3:15.
6. Do not tell a person he is saved. That is the Holy Spirit's work. Show how to be saved.
   1 *Jno.* 5:10; *Jer.* 6:14; 1 *Cor.* 2:10-13; *Rom.* 8:16.
7. Feel the necessity, and prove the power of prayer.
   Jer. 33:3; *Rom.* 8:26, 27; *Jas.* 5:16; *Heb.* 11:6.

INDEX OF TITLES AND FIRST LINES.

A charge to keep I have 111
A child of the King........................ 124
A little talk with Jesus 88
A pilgrim and a stranger 155
A pilgrim I journey 217
Abide with me 117
Abundantly able to save 70
Adeste Fideles 226
Ah, my heart 64
Alas, and did 27
All hail the power 88
All for Jesus 82
All-victorious love 109
Almost persuaded 178
Almost saved 176
Although I wandered....................... 151
Am I a soldier of the cross?.............. 237
Angels hovering round 243
Are you coming home?...................... 61
Are you ready for the 34
Are you ready?............................ 181
Are you trusting?......................... 63
Are you weary?............................ 59
Art thou lost? 81
Ashamed of Jesus 102

Beautiful words 231
Beautiful river 202
Belmont 32
Believing and receiving................... 127
Beulah Land 148
Blest be the tie.......................... 141
Bright is the day-star.................... 129
Brightly gleams our banner................ 160
Breaking through the clouds 192
By faith the Lamb of God.................. 15

Calling for you........................... 46
Calling us away 204
Called to the feast 14
Calvary 20
Christ, the solid Rock 144
Christ's vicarious sacrifice 27
Christian soldiers' battle-song........... 108
Cleansing wave............................ 145
Come 244
Come, all ye saints 197
Come, believing 47
Come, every soul.......................... 54
Come, halting sinner 55
Come, let us all 238
Come, O my God, the promise seal 115
Come, one and all 161
Come, poor sinners........................ 78

Come, thou Fount 96
Come, thou long-expected 221
Come to Jesus 65
Come to me 51
Come, we that love........................ 232
Come with hearts and voices 248
Come, ye sinners, come to-day 71
Come, ye sinners, poor and needy.......... 79
Coming to-day 18
Coming, yes, we're coming 11
Companionship with Jesus 134
Consecration prayer 122
Coronation................................ 33

Death-bells tolling 214
Do you hear the Saviour?.................. 12
Don't go near the bar-room 227
Down at the cross 143
Draw me nearer 147

Eternity! where? 177
Every day and hour 106

Fall into line............................ 167
From every stormy wind 103
Full salvation 156

Galilee................................... 22
Gathering home 179
Gethsemane 26
Give me the wings 204
Gloria Patri 123
Glory be to the Father 123
Glory to His Name 143
God is calling yet........................ 235
God is coming 72
God is love............................... 238
God loved the world 78
Go tell the world......................... 158
Go to Jesus 68
Go ye out to meet Him..................... 72
Guide me 95

Hallelujah for the cross.................. 49
Happy day................................. 140
Happy in the Lord 156
Happy in the love 129
Happy all the day 237
Hark! the song 185
Hark! there comes a whisper 13
Hark! the voice of Jesus calling 70
Have mercy, Lord, on me................... 87
Have you been to Jesus?................... 234
Have you on the Lord believed? 80

INDEX.

He leadeth me	137
He loved me so	15
He has come	130
He took me in	151
Hear the call	171
Heaven my home	217
Heirs to the kingdom	158
His grace is free	10
Holy Spirit, faithful Guide	119
Home at last	185
How firm a foundation	223
How prospers thy soul ?	212
How sad it would be	173
How sweet the Name	110
How sweet the call	11
I am free	136
I am saved, yes, I'm saved	127
I am so glad	241
I am Thine	147
I am listening	12
I can, I will, I do believe	84
I do believe	108
I gave my life	76
I have been at the fountain	157
I have a Saviour	138
I have a song	139
I have given my heart to Jesus	244
I hear Thy welcome voice	37
I heard the voice of Jesus say	32
I know that my Redeemer lives	126
I know that my Redeemer lives	146
I love to think	230
I need Thee every hour	114
I praise the Lord that one like me	4
I shall be satisfied	187
I want to be a worker	159
I will	245
I will sing of	39
I will, I do believe	115
I'm glad salvation's free	229
I'm going home	201
In the field of Christian duty	166
In the Christian's home	183
In the cross of Christ	219
In the morning	208
Into a tent	160
Is there a sinner	60
Is it well with thee	212
It is well with my soul	152
It is good to be here	153
I've found a Friend	7
I've reached the land	148
Jesus, and shall it ever be	102
Jesus bids you come	43
Jesus Christ has	40
Jesus from His throne	30
Jesus, keep me near the cross	105
Jesus lifted up	30
Jesus, lover of my soul	121
Jesus, my Lord, to Thee	83
Jesus, my Saviour	9
Jesus of Nazareth passeth by	16
Jesus the water of life	62
Jesus, Thine all-victorious love	100
Jesus is calling	45
Jesus is calling you now	66
Jesus is coming	8
Jesus is pleading	52
Jesus is passing	60
Jesus is waiting to save	73
Jesus loves poor sinners	31
Jesus saves	35
Jesus, the loving Shepherd	74
Jesus, when He left the sky	236
Jesus will forgive	71
Jesus will give you rest	53
Just as I am	84, 101
Just now believe	75
Kneeling, pleading, waiting	87
Lead, kindly light	89
Lead me, Saviour	86
Let Him in	58
Like a star of the morning	125
List, the Spirit	48
Little ones like me	234
Look away to the cross	69
Look and live	67
Look to Jesus	67
Lord's Prayer	120
Lord, I hear	113
Lord, dismiss us	97
Lo ! the day of God	171
Loving Saviour, hear	91
Love divine	93
Lux Benigna	89
Marching to glory	248
Martyn	1 1
Meet me there	191
Mercy is boundless	42
More love to Thee	91
More to follow	89
Motto song	247
My faith looks up to Thee	183
My Father is rich	124
My heart's desire	104
My heavenly home	201
My hope is built	144
My Jesus, I would ne'er	26
My little friends	247
My precious Bible	125
My Redeemer	59
Near the cross	105
Nearer the cross	142
Nearer, my God, to Thee	90
Nearer my home	207
No night in heaven	191
No room in heaven	173
Not my own	85
Now just a word	233
Now the chains	136
O, blessed fellowship	134
O, bliss of the purified	112
O come, all ye faithful	226
O come, let us praise the Redeemer	6
O, come to the Saviour	46
O, for a heart to praise	116
O, for a thousand	270
O, Galilee	22
O, happy day	149
O, how happy are we	154
O, how happy are they	153
O, love beyond	10
O, never be weary	102
O, now I see the cleansing wave	145
O, sing to me	228
O, think of the home	206
O, Thou who earnest	104
O, 'tis wonderful	131
O, weep for the fallen	224
O, when shall I sweep	195
O, what amazing	56
Oh, come to the Saviour	46
Oh, do not let the Word depart	215

170

INDEX.

Oh, have you not seen	69
Oh, sing to me of heaven	228
Oh, now I see	145
Oh, word of words	244
On Calvary's brow	20
On the happy golden shore	191
Once again	47
Once I thought	140
Once more my soul	245
One by one	180
One sweetly solemn	207
Only trust Him	54
Onward, Christian soldiers	168
Our Father, which art	120
Our glad jubilee	1
Our Lord is now	180
Our loved ones in heaven	197
Our souls are in	211
Out on the desert	18
Over there	206
O er Jordan's dark	263
Parting hymn	97
Pass me not	107
Pentecostal power	118
Pleading with thee	49
Praise the Redeemer	6
Precious Jesus, oh	14
Precious Jesus, Thou hast	156
Portuguese Hymn	223
Rescue the perishing	165
Responsive service	249
Rest for the weary	183
Resting at the cross	133
Return, O wanderer	33
Ring the bells	242
Rock of ages	29
Saviour, lead me	86
Saviour, like a shepherd	100
Saviour, more than life	106
Saviour, though long I	132
Safe on the rock	135
Safe in Thy arms	128
Save me at the cross	94
Scripture passages	250
Seeking for me	9
Seeking to save	44
Shall I meet you	186
Shall we meet in heaven	194
Shall we gather	202
Shall we meet beyond	210
Shout for joy	214
Since I've trusted	140
Since I have been redeemed	133
Sing on, ye joyful pilgrims	2
Sing, O sing the love of Jesus	3
Sing them over again	231
Sing of His mighty love	112
Softly and tenderly	45
Some one knocking	24
Soon the evening shadows	181
Sound the battle cry	170
Sowing in the morning	103
Speaking for Jesus	234
Sweet by and by	199
Sweet rest at home	203
Take me as I am	83
Take my life and let it be	122
Take the Name of Jesus	218
Tell it to Jesus	59
Tell me more	23
Tenderly the Shepherd	44
Thanks be to Jesus	42
That beautiful world	198
The bleeding Lamb	40
The blessed feast	78
The bright forever	191
The coming Bridegroom	34
The cross it standeth fast	210
The crowning day	180
The crucifixion	21
The door of God's mercy is open	172
The field of Christian duty	166
The gipsy boy	100
The glorious fountain	17
The gospel invitation	79
The gospel ship	77
The great physician	41
The Judgment Day	182
The Lily of the Valley	7
The loving Shepherd	74
The mercy-seat	103
The name of Jesus	110
The name of Jesus	239
The new song	2 9
The numberless host	196
The pearly gate	172
The precious Name	218
The prize is set	205
The Rose of Sharon	25
The Saviour speaks	75
The Spirit and the bride	50
The Spirit, O sinner	225
The three warnings	225
The universal call	50
The water of life	62
There are angels	243
There is a beautiful world	198
There is a green hill	19
There is a fountain	17
There's a land	199
There's a Rose	25
There's a stranger	88
There's a wideness	220
They're gathering homeward	179
This year for Jesus	161
Thousands stand to-day in sorrow	222
Thy precious fold	132
Tidings, happy tidings	67
Till Jesus comes	211
'Tis known on earth and heaven too	23
'Tis the very same power	118
Toiling up the way	189
To the cross of Christ	133
To the rescue	214
To that city will you go	184
Triumph by and by	205
Trusting Jesus	63
Until I heard of	108
Wake, wake the song	1
Wait a little while	209
Waiting at the pool	222
We are pilgrims	208
We are marching up	189
We have heard a joyful sound	83
We praise Thee	5
We shall reap by and by	162
We will sing the praise of Jesus	188
Weary and thirsty	49
Welcome to glory	195
What a Friend	95
What a gathering	200
What means this eager	16
When I shall wake	187

171

INDEX.

When I survey	21	Will you be saved to-night	52
When I was far away and lost	131	Will you come	53
When peace like a river	152	With tearful eyes	51
When the harvest is past	175	Whoever receiveth	70
When the King comes in	174	Whosoever	4
When the pearly gates unfold	246	Why do you linger in darkness	73
When shall Thy love constrain	229	Why do you wait	66
When we all get home	198	Why not to-night	215
When we all gather home	200	Why I love Jesus	150
When we enter the portals	106	Would you know why	150
Where is my wandering boy	216	Work, for the night	164
Where the jasper walls	184	Work to-day	164
Will you be washed	48	Working, O Christ, with Thee	92

INDEX OF SUBJECTS.

Praise	1– 6	Work	158–166
Jesus	7– 41	Warfare	167–171
Invitation and Assurance	42– 81	Warning	172–178
Consecration	82– 85	Death and Judgment	179–182
Prayer and Trust	86–123	Heaven	183–211
Christian Experience	124–157	Miscellaneous	212–250

www.ingramcontent.com/pod-product-compliance
Lightning Source LLC
Chambersburg PA
CBHW032155160426
43197CB00008B/923